# Scratch Programming for Beginners

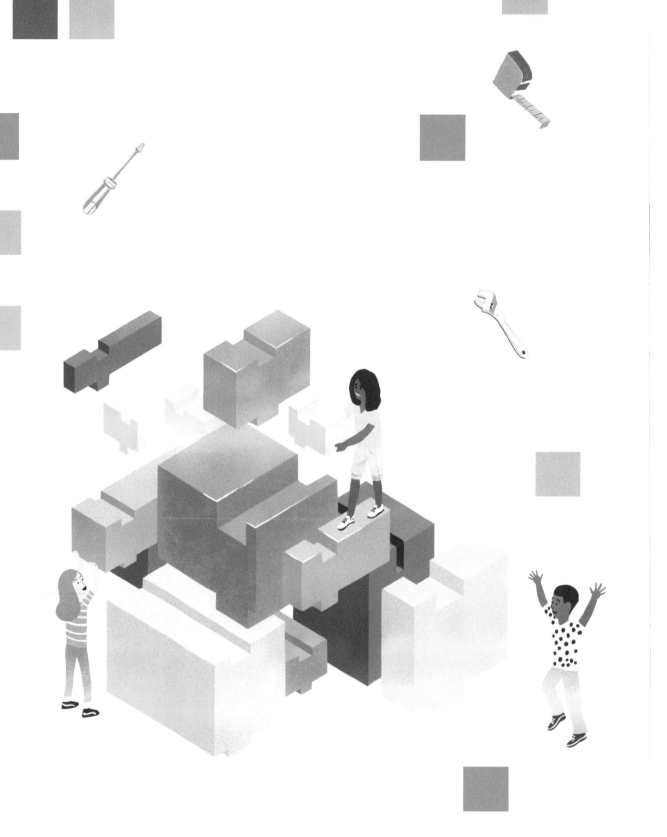

# Scratch Programming for Beginners

## A Kid's Guide to Coding Fundamentals

Raina Burditt, MS, MA

Illustrations by Ryan Johnson

ROCKRIDGE
PRESS

For general information on our other products and services or to obtain technical support, please contact our Customer Care Department within the United States at (866) 744-2665, or outside the United States at (510) 253-0500.

Rockridge Press publishes its books in a variety of electronic and print formats. Some content that appears in print may not be available in electronic books, and vice versa.

Interior and Cover Designer: Suzanne LaGasa
Art Producer: Sara Feinstein
Editor: Caitlin Prim
Production Editor: Jenna Dutton
Illustrations © 2020 Ryan Johnson. Author photo courtesy of © Grant Burke.

ISBN: Print 978-1-64739-638-1 | eBook 978-1-64739-639-8
R0

To my daughter, Claire.
May you never lose your sense of wonder.

# Contents

# How to Use This Book

**Are you interested in coding?** This book is going to teach you how to think and solve problems like a computer programmer! We'll start with an introduction to the basics of coding and then take some first steps into using Scratch, a fun coding language. Next, you will discover important coding concepts that will become the tools in your toolbox for making programs. These chapters will lead you through three different activities, each a little more challenging than the one before it. After we finish building your toolbox, we'll work together to make a really cool game where you'll fight off a fire-breathing dragon so you can return a wizard's wand! Then you'll feel confident and ready to create anything you can imagine!

This book also includes several important sections at the end. You can flip ahead anytime to check out **Bug Hunting: Troubleshooting Tips** (page 164). This is a list of common mistakes people make when writing code along with tips on how to fix them. There's also a **Glossary** (page 166), where you can look up new words you come across in this book. When you've finished all of the activities and made the final game, check out **Code for the Road** (page 163) for great ideas for what to do next!

Make sure you ask a parent or guardian for permission before logging into Scratch or downloading it from the Internet. That's just a good safety tip to remember anytime you are going to a new site online.

The good news: kids are awesome coders. You're smart and curious, and you enjoy using a computer, right? That's all you need to get started.

So, are you ready to learn how to code and learn this cool new language? Great—let's start building your toolbox of skills!

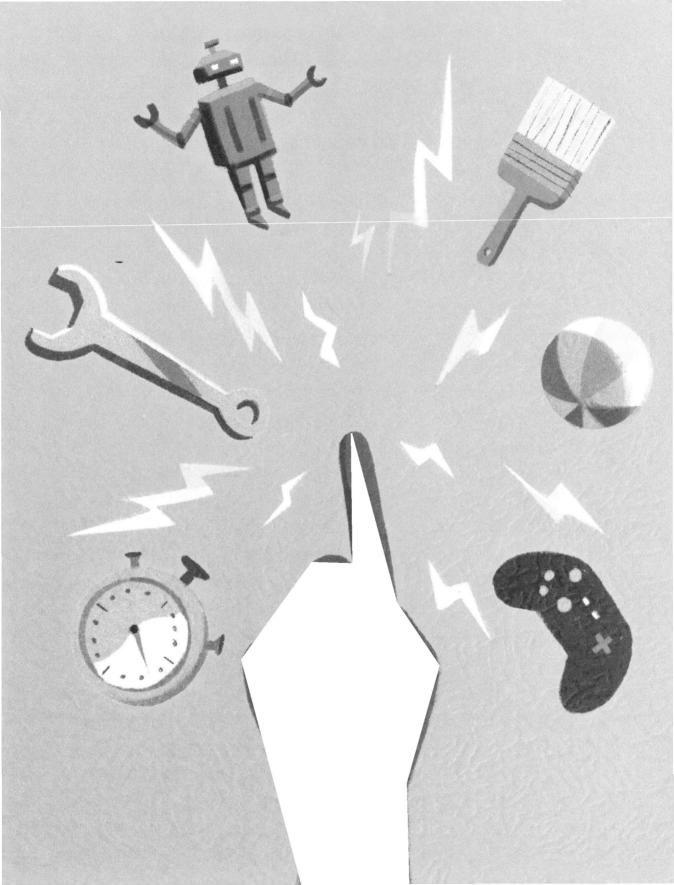

# Welcome to Programming!

Programming is really fun—but first you might be wondering, *What exactly is programming?*

Programming is basically just us humans telling our computers what to do. You are already telling computers what to do all the time. Didn't you tell your computer to open up your saved report so you could print it for school? Well, yes—but there's a whole lot of other directions your computer needed to print that paper.

First, when you clicked on the icon for your report, your computer knew it needed to open up that exact file and display your report.

If you decided to type a few more sentences, your computer needed to know what letter to display for each key that you tapped on.

Even the simple act of moving your mouse across the screen to click on the print button required lots of directions for your computer.

These instructions that you don't see, but your computer is following, are referred to as **code**. This is why people who are programming are also said to be "coding." They create all those instructions that your computer follows. Whenever you interact with an electronic device, it is constantly checking its code, following all the directions that someone has programmed for it. It doesn't have a brain like you or me, so it depends on this code to tell it what to do.

So why should you care about all that code? It's not something you can actually *see* happening. You just get to kick back and enjoy all the great stuff that it's making your computer do.

But haven't you ever wished that your computer could do something *else* or maybe just do the same thing but *better*? Like, instead of clicking the arrow keys to make your ninja character move in a game, wouldn't it be cool if the ninja just followed your mouse instead?

If you know how to **program**, *you* can decide what instructions you want your computer to follow! You can make it behave any way that you want. *You* get to be the creator. It's kind of like the difference between a reading a story and *writing* a story. Sure, reading a story is fun, but how much cooler is it to use your imagination to make up your *own* story and then share it with your friends?

Learning to code doesn't mean you have to grow up to become a professional programmer, although you can if you want to! Learning to code is valuable for *anyone* because it teaches you how to take apart a problem and solve it.

Creating your own programs will also help you learn the process of design, which means starting with an idea you have in your head and making it actually happen! Most importantly, programming helps you really understand what goes on inside the technologies that you use all the time.

This book is a guide for kids who have never coded before but who are ready to learn how to think like a coder!

# What Are Programs?

A program is a list of instructions (or code) that tells an electronic device what to do. Those instructions are listed in a specific order so the device can understand what tasks you want it to perform. These directions must be broken into small, clear steps.

Imagine trying to teach an alien how to open a door if they had never seen a door before. You couldn't just say, "Turn the knob and push it open." The alien would be full of questions like "Which part is the knob? Turn it with what? Where do I push?"

The alien has never been to Earth before, so they would be super confused. You really have to give this poor alien every single detail of how to open a door. Directions for your confused alien might look like this:

1. Place your hand on the circular metal object that is located on the middle left-hand side of the large wooden rectangle.

2. Rotate the metal object with your hand 90 degrees to the right.

3. Hold the metal object in the same position while also pushing the large wooden rectangle forward with your other hand.

4. Step forward through the opening.

5. Release your hand from the circular metal object.

This is exactly how computers behave. They are like an alien who cannot do even the tiniest thing without very clear instructions. Programs are the directions that help them understand what we humans want them to do. That means when you are writing a program, you have to assume that your computer knows absolutely nothing! It needs *you* to break down every action into very small steps.

# 1 Every program is made up of a combination of five basic parts:

## INPUT

**Input** is information that is entered into the computer. Imagine you are using a calculator to do a math problem. If you type in 2 + 2, that's your input.

## OUTPUT

**Output** is information that is provided by the computer. Think of that calculator again. Once you type in your math problem of 2 + 2, it will give you the output of 4.

## MATH

You know this one! **Math** is the operation that the computer will perform for you. In this case, the calculator has to know how to add 2 and 2 together so that it will be able to give you the correct output of 4.

## CONDITIONAL EXECUTION

**Conditional execution** means there are different paths, or conditions, that can change depending on what the input is. If you input 2 + 2, then the calculator will output the number 4. If you input 5 + 5, then the calculator will output the number 10. Those are two separate possible paths. You can also think of these as rules that the computer must follow.

## REPETITION

**Repetition** is when a set of steps is repeated. In a program, the computer can repeat a set of instructions a certain number of times or until it gets a certain result. For example, your calculator can repeat your instruction to keep adding whatever numbers you are pushing *until* you push another type of button, like the = sign. Then it follows new instructions, which are to complete the math operation for your problem, clear out those numbers from its display screen, and then display the output, which is the solution to your math problem.

# The Basic Coding Concepts

There are many different coding languages, but they all use some of the same basic tools to solve problems and build programs. The concepts you'll learn in this book will be the "tools" in your coding toolbox. You'll learn that each tool can do lots of different things for you, but some tools will be better for certain tasks. For example, a hammer is great for hammering in nails but not so great for cutting a board—you'd need to pull out your saw for that one! Once you learn how to use your coding tools, you'll understand how programmers think and how you can use many different tools together to make bigger, more complex programs. Then you'll be on your way to building your very own programs!

## These concepts are:

### VARIABLES

**Variables** are a tool that you will use to store information. You can change the value of that information whenever you need to. For example, you could use a variable to keep track of the score in a game.

### CONDITIONS

Conditions help us create the conditional executions we discussed earlier. You can create different possible paths, just like a choose-your-own-adventure story! For example, if the user clicks the frog, it will jump up and down. But if the user clicks the pond, the frog will jump into the water. Those are two possible paths that the user can take.

### DATA TYPES AND DATA STRUCTURES

**Data** is just a fancy word for information. Data types and data structures are ways to organize our information in the program, just like you might organize how you want your materials laid out on your desk at school.

### EVENT HANDLING

**Events** are the triggers for your code—they make it go. Once you set off an event (like clicking an icon with your mouse), then the computer knows to follow the set of directions (or code) that is attached to that event.

### LOOPS

**Loops** are how you create the repetition we talked about earlier. You can use a loop to make your program repeat the same steps multiple times. Imagine you wrote code that would make a ball bounce across the screen. If you wanted that to happen 100 times, it would be much easier to put a "repeat 100 times loop" around your code than to actually rewrite that code 100 times!

These are the main concepts of coding, and they are the tools every programmer uses, no matter which programming language they are writing in. If you are feeling a little confused so far, don't worry! Once you start actually placing code in a program, a lot of these terms will make more sense.

## Talk Like a Programmer: Words to Know

Now that we have our tools, let's learn some words that will be important to know later.

### RUN

The code is just the instructions for the computer. "Running" the code is when the computer actually performs those instructions. A programmer might say, "Let's **run** this program and see if it's working."

### ALGORITHM

An **algorithm** is any logical group of steps used to perform a task or solve a problem. This sounds a lot like our definition of a program. But actually, the algorithm is the *idea*. The program is the actual code to make that idea happen. Following an algorithm is like following a recipe. The cake you get by completing your recipe is your program. A programmer might say, "I need to think of a good algorithm for my program."

## SCRIPT

When programmers talk about a **script**, they are referring to code that's written in a specific programming language. A programmer might say, "I'm working on a script that will make the spaceship move faster." Since we will be using a specific programming language, Scratch, the code that you will write can be called a script.

## FUNCTION

A **function** is a piece of code that doesn't run unless you give it a specific input. For example, your calculator will not run the code to calculate your math problem until you push the = button. Until that moment, the code is a *function* that is waiting for its trigger, or event. A programmer might say, "This function won't run unless you click on the green button."

## OPERATORS

**Operators** are a special type of function that allows you to make mathematical calculations like adding and subtracting. They can also make logical comparisons such as greater than (>) or less than (<). A programmer might say, "If the score is greater than 10, then I want the *You Won* screen to pop up. I will use an operator to do that."

# Why Scratch?

By now you might be thinking, *Why should I start with Scratch?*

   This book will teach you how to think like a programmer so you can feel confident trying *any* programming language. However, the language we are going to use to introduce you to programming is Scratch. This is a programming language developed by teachers, students, and researchers at Massachusetts Institute of Technology (MIT).

   We chose Scratch because it's a fun language that was written just for kids! To create code, Scratch uses blocks that fit together like Legos, which makes it a *visual* language. That means you can see how your code affects the program as you are building it—no waiting around!

Scratch contains a large menu of code blocks with all sorts of possible instructions. Each piece of code is a block that contains just one command. The blocks snap onto one another to form long stacks of blocks. As you snap each code block together, you are forming a list of step-by-step directions, or a *program*.

People around the world love Scratch because it was designed to be *fun*! It has lots of cool characters, backdrops, and sounds for you to play with.

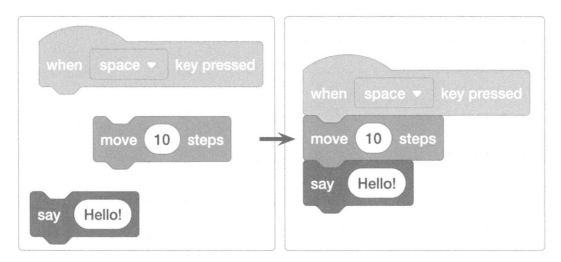

The directions above say: When the space bar is pressed, move the character forward by 10 steps, and say "Hello."

Many programming languages use a lot of typed commands. But in Scratch, building a program is more about creating a logical path. In fact, there is *very* little typing in Scratch. This is good news because it means your program will not fail because you put a comma in the wrong place or misspelled a word. You'll still have errors in your programs (we all do!), and you'll need to use creativity and problem-solving to fix them, but you will not get stuck because of a simple typo. Phew!

Even though we will be using only one programming language, Scratch, you are learning coding basics that can be used for *any* coding language. Working with Scratch will also help you build great troubleshooting skills and sharpen your ability to think about problems in a logical way. By the end of this book, you'll have a great understanding of Scratch and will be able to make all kinds of fun programs. But more importantly, you'll understand basic coding concepts so that you can start thinking and *creating* like a programmer. Then when you are ready to start exploring other programming languages, you'll already have a great toolbox full of tools to help you learn much faster.

## What Can Scratch Do?

You may be thinking that programming in Scratch is just a way to make games, but really that's just the beginning of what Scratch can do! Kids and adults all over the world use Scratch every day to solve problems, make art, write music, tell stories, create simulations, and much, *much* more. Scratch users have also created a free online community where they can share their projects and learn from each other's code. It's like a gigantic group project!

# 2

# Scratch: The Basics

Wow! You learned *a lot* in the last chapter about programming, but I bet you're ready to stop reading about coding and start *doing* some coding, right? So, let's get Scratch set up on your computer.

To do this, you will need an Internet connection. If you don't have regular access to the Internet, don't worry—you will have the option of working without Internet once you have the program downloaded.

# How to Install Scratch

The very first version of Scratch was released in 2007. MIT released an updated version, Scratch 2.0, in 2013. Its latest version, Scratch 3.0, was released in 2019.

That's a lot of versions, but don't worry! Although updates are constantly being made, the basics of using Scratch always stay the same. Even when Scratch 4.0 is released, you will have no problem using the program. Scratch is available in an **online** format, which means you can use the Internet to create and store your programs. It's also available in an **offline** format, called Scratch Desktop, which means it can run as a program on your computer, no Internet required! Both programs work the same way. If you have a strong Internet connection, try the online version. If you want to be able to code without Internet, try Scratch Desktop.

## Offline

To download the offline version of Scratch, you will need to type this address into a web browser: **scratch.mit.edu/download**.

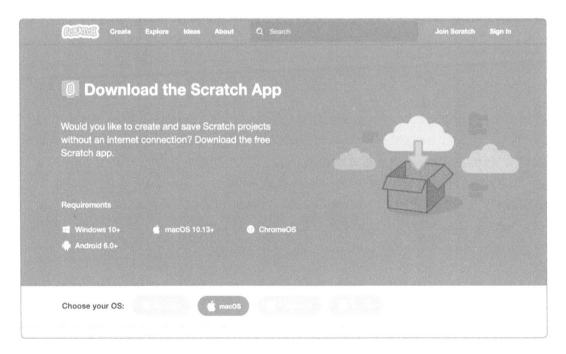

There are currently four versions of Scratch available, based on the type of computer you're using. The one listed for Windows is what you will need if you are working on a PC. The macOS version is for Macs. There is also a version for Chromebooks and a version for Android tablets.

Don't worry—Scratch looks and works the same no matter what type of computer you are using.

Remember to ask an adult if you need help deciding which version you need. They can also help you with the download process. Downloading Scratch takes only a couple of minutes!

Once the download is ready, just click the new Scratch icon to launch Scratch Desktop. It will take you to a new project screen. Then you're ready to start coding!

Since Scratch Desktop will work without needing the Internet, it's a good choice for users who don't want to worry about a slow Internet speed or the possibility of the website being down.

## Online

If you'd rather use Scratch online, the web-based interface will work on any browser and on any type of computer. The Scratch website will also save your work in the cloud, which means you can work on a program from a computer at school and then continue working on the same program from your computer at home. As long as you have Internet, you can access online Scratch from anywhere!

To get started with Scratch online, type this address into a web browser: **scratch.mit.edu**.

Start by clicking "Join Scratch" in the upper right-hand corner.

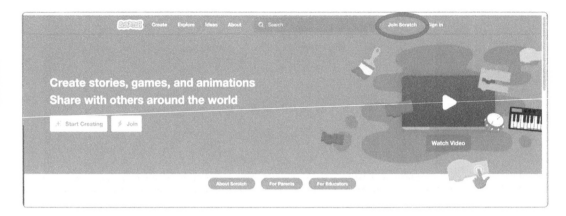

You will be asked to create an account and will need to answer a few questions. You'll also need an email address to create an account.

The online version has one extra step before you are ready to code. You'll need to click on "Create" in the top menu bar to start a new project in Scratch.

When you start a new project, it will already have a title, "Untitled," which you can see across the top in the menu bar. Just click and type inside this box to create your own title.

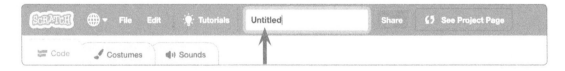

You can also share your project with the online Scratch community. To share your project, just click the orange "Share" button in the top menu bar. Once it's shared, you can copy the URL (the Internet address of your project) from your web browser and send it to friends and family so they can view your work online. Pretty cool, right?

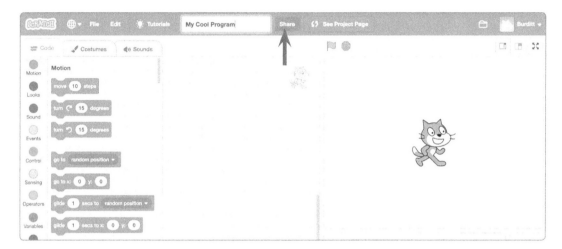

# Saving Your Stuff

Now that we're in Scratch, the next thing we'll learn is how to save our code. When you've worked really hard to make something cool, you definitely don't want to lose it! There are a couple of differences in how you save with the Scratch Desktop versus the online version of Scratch.

# Online

If you are working in the online version, your work will auto-save every few minutes. If you look on the top right of the menu bar and you see the words "Save Now," that means it has *not* auto-saved your most recent work yet. Click it! Then your latest code will be saved.

If you don't see the "Save Now" option on the menu bar and you want to be extra sure that all of your progress is saved, then select "File" from the menu bar and then "Save Now" from the drop-down menu.

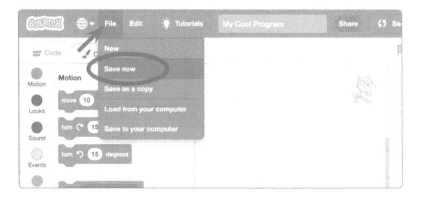

Notice that you have some other options under "File":

***New*** will start a brand-new program.

***Save as a copy*** will duplicate your program. This can be useful if you want to make some big changes to your code but are worried that you might end up wanting to go back to the way it was before the changes. Just make a copy, and then you will still have the original version of the program saved.

**Load from your computer** is how you can upload a program that was made with Scratch Desktop into the online version. Many people use both the online and offline versions, switching between them as needed.

**Save to your computer** is how you can download a program from the online version so you can open it with Scratch Desktop later.

## Offline

To save your work when you are using Scratch Desktop, select "File" from the top menu bar and then "Save to your computer" from the drop-down menu. Save your program in a folder on your computer. Make sure you remember where you put it!

Notice that you have some other options under "File":

**New** will start a brand-new program.

**Load from your computer** is how you get back to your saved work. Just open up the program that you saved in a folder on your computer. You can also click here to upload a program that you downloaded from the online version of Scratch.

# Gathering Your Tools

Now let's explore all the tools you will be using to make your creations in Scratch.

Make sure you have Scratch opened up on your computer. If you are using the online version, remember to click on "Create" to get to the new project page.

Notice that you have a list of possible commands on the left-hand side of the screen. This is your **code menu**. The big white space in the middle of your screen is the **script editor**. You will drag **code blocks** from the code menu into this big white space to write your program. The box on the upper right-hand side is your **stage**. This is where you can immediately see what your program looks like. For example, if you write code that makes the cat jump up and down, you'll be able to see it happening right here! Speaking of the cat, every time you start a new project, you will always see a preloaded character, Scratch the cat. We call characters like this one **sprites**.

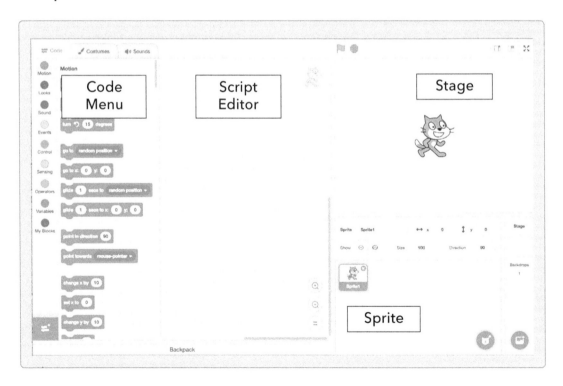

## The Sprites

Sprites are characters and props that you can use in your program. They can move, talk, dance, draw, play music—they can do anything you want them to do! There are many preloaded sprites to use in Scratch, but you can also create your own sprites. You can do this by drawing a sprite in the program or by uploading an image from the Internet and turning it into a sprite.

You'll see Scratch the cat every time you begin a new project, but you don't have to use the cat unless you want to. There's a whole world of sprites to explore, and they're all pretty cool!

## The Stage

The box on the upper right-hand side is your stage. This is where you will see a preview of your program. If you write code that makes the cat do a cartwheel, this is where you will see it happen. Usually, you will click the green flag above the stage to run your program, and you can click the red stop sign to stop your program.

## Creating Scripts

Remember that when you are writing a set of directions in a programming language, we call it a script. The big white space in the middle of your screen is your script editor. To start writing a script, you'll click and drag the colored code blocks from the code menu on the left. Code blocks connect together to form longer lists of directions, or scripts, for your program. You can have many different scripts within a program.

# Code Blocks

One of the reasons Scratch is such a fun programming language is because it is a *visual* language. It uses colorful blocks to represent the code. Certain types of code share the same color to help you find what you need quickly. The different shapes show you how the commands connect to one another. Let's explore them.

**‹ MOTION BLOCKS**

These dark blue code blocks are all about making your sprites move around the stage. Not only can you make a sprite move, but you can also control *how* it moves. Will the sprite pop up instantly in a new spot, or will it glide there? Will it flip to face a different direction, or will it spin in circles? You decide!

**‹ LOOKS BLOCKS**

These dark purple code blocks allow you to change the appearance of your sprite with costume changes or by making it grow or shrink. You can also make your sprites use word bubbles to talk or think!

**‹ SOUND BLOCKS**

These light-purple code blocks add an audio track to your programs. You can use preloaded songs and sound effects from Scratch or record your own!

**‹ EVENTS BLOCKS**

These yellow code blocks are how you create the events that we discussed in chapter 1. They are the triggers that will let the computer know when it is time to follow a certain set of directions or code. For example, you can use an event to make the cat meow or bark or dance every time you click on him.

**《 CONTROL BLOCKS**

These light-orange code blocks allow you to adjust the timing between each of your commands. They also allow you to create loops to repeat sets of directions. Finally, there are "if-then" statements that let you create conditions, or rules, for how you want your program to run.

**《 SENSING BLOCKS**

These light-blue code blocks are used to detect or "sense" things. They help the computer know where your mouse pointer is or whether two sprites are touching. This helps you set up conditions for what you want to happen if, for example, two sprites collide. Ouch!

**《 OPERATOR BLOCKS**

These green code blocks allow you to make mathematical calculations and comparisons. This helps you tell the computer how to respond if, for example, the sprite's health points have gone down to zero. I'm thinking the game would be over then—what do *you* think?

**《 VARIABLES**

These orange code blocks are used to create variables and change their values. If you want to make a game that can keep score, you'll need a variable to store that information.

2

# Hacker Hints

**1** When you are navigating all the possible options in the code menu, you can click on the colorful little circles on the far-left side of the screen to quickly jump to different sections. For example, if you know you are looking for sensing code, just click on the light-blue sensing circle, and the menu will jump to that part of the list for you. It's a great shortcut to quickly find the code you need!

**2** Notice that your code blocks come in different shapes. These shapes tell you how they can fit together. For example, most event code blocks have a curved top. They *begin* scripts because that curved top cannot connect to anything. But look at the little peg on the bottom of an event block. Some blocks have a matching hole on top. That means those two pieces of code can connect to one another.

Some code blocks have an oval or a hexagon shape inside them. Only the code blocks that have the same shape can fit into those code locks. You will have so much fun testing out all the options!

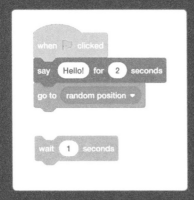

# Bugs

Coding can include a lot of trial and error. Sometimes you will write a script and discover that the program does *not* do what you were expecting. What then?

When a program isn't running properly, programmers have to look back through all of the code and check for the mistake, or **bug**, that is causing the problem.

Usually the bug is just a logical error. Maybe you wanted to write a program where a frog says hello and then jumps up on a table, but you accidentally put those commands in the wrong place. Now the table is on top of the frog! When something like that happens, you'll need to read back carefully through your code to see where the problem is. Fixing problems with your code is called **debugging**.

Bugs don't just happen to kids. Even professional programmers make mistakes in their code, so they are always testing their programs for bugs. In fact, it's a good idea to run your program every time you add or change something in your script, just to make sure the new code works the way you were hoping. It's a lot easier to test after each new command is added than to try to figure out where something might have gone wrong in a long list of code blocks!

Let's roll up our sleeves, because in the next chapter we're going to dive into our toolbox and start creating!

## A "Buggy" History!

Want to hear a funny story? The *very* first computer bug error was a REAL bug! That's right! Back in 1946, one of the first computers ever made was malfunctioning because a moth had gotten stuck inside the machine. That's where the term "bug" comes from!

# 3

# Making It Move

In the last two chapters, we went over the fundamental concepts of programming and learned how to navigate Scratch. Now it's time to dive in and actually do some coding! Our first step is learning how to make sprites move around our stage.

If you already have a new project open in Scratch, then you're ready to roll. If not, open up Scratch Desktop, or if you are in the online version, click "Create" on the top menu bar.

# Choosing a Sprite

Go ahead and delete Scratch the cat. The cat pops up automatically when you start a new program, but you don't need the cat right now. Just click on the little trash can icon next to the cat's thumbnail image under the stage. Go ahead and ditch that cat! (Don't worry—the cat won't mind.)

To bring in a new sprite, click on the blue cat icon under the stage—it will turn green when you select it. There you go!

You will see a whole library of options pop up. Cool, right?

Notice that the sprites are listed alphabetically. There's also a search bar for sprites in the top-left corner of the screen. For this activity, let's choose Llama.

Isn't he cute? When you are ready for more sprites, you can follow the same steps to bring in whomever you want!

# Creating Movement

Being able to move our sprites around is super important! With movement, we can build exciting animations and games.

## Coordinates

First, it's important to understand that your sprite is on a **coordinate plane**. A coordinate plane is also called a graph. The line that goes up and down is the **y-axis**, and the line that goes left to right is the **x-axis**. Each position on the coordinate plane has an x-value and a y-value based on where it is located. These values are called **coordinates**.

Whoa, that all sounded really complicated, right? Don't worry—it's much easier in action. The coordinates just let us map out an exact location. Right now, the very center of Llama is positioned on the spot where the two lines intersect. That is a special spot where the x-axis value is 0 and the y-axis value is also 0. That means the coordinates for Llama are (0,0). We always list the x-coordinate first and then the y-coordinate. Yep, they go in the same order as the letters "x" and "y" in the alphabet.

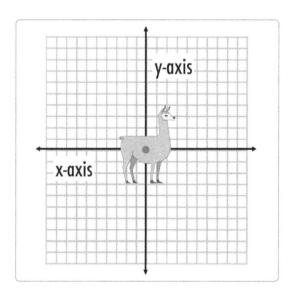

If Llama moves left on the x-axis from the intersection of the two lines, the value of his x-coordinate will be a negative number because he is going to numbers that are *less* than zero. If he moves to the right of the intersection, he is going *above* zero, so the x-value will be a positive number. In the same way, moving up on the y-axis from the (0,0) intersection means the y-coordinate will be a positive number, and moving down on the y-axis means the y-coordinate will be a negative number.

In the image below, count how many boxes Llama has moved to the right along the x-axis. Five, right? That means his x-coordinate now equals 5. Now count how many boxes down he has moved on the y-axis. Did you get 4? Great! But remember, he moved *below* the intersection, which is zero, so his y-axis now equals *negative* 4.

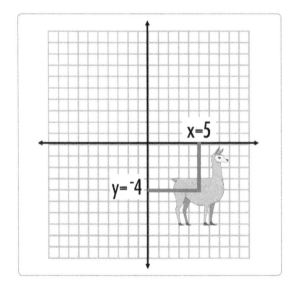

When you move Llama around the stage in Scratch, imagine him moving around on the coordinate plane we just looked at. Go ahead and click on Llama and try placing him in a few different positions. Every time he moves, notice that his x- and y-values change. You can see exactly which coordinate he is currently placed on by looking at the numbers right below the stage. There are even helpful arrows to remind you that the x-axis moves left and right and the y-axis moves up and down.

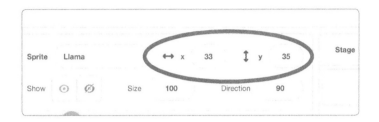

Now let's look at some code options. Go to the very top of your code menu for the **motion** section. Do you see that some of the blocks have x- or y-values listed? Those numbers will automatically update to wherever your sprite is currently positioned.

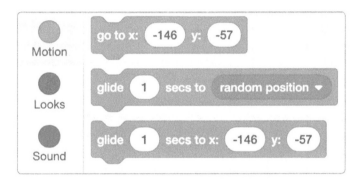

Let's test this! Try clicking and moving Llama to different spots on the stage. Watch how the x- and y-values change in your list of motion code blocks. This is super useful when it comes to planning out your sprite's movements. It's always best to move your sprite where you want it to be and *then* select your motion block. That way, you know the coordinates will be correct, and the code will place them exactly where you want them. You can also click in the boxes and change the numbers yourself.

# Directions

At the moment, Llama is standing up nicely, but suppose he were to trip and fall flat on his face. Now, we wouldn't *want* that to happen to our nice llama, but let's just suppose it *could* happen. Luckily, your motion code also contains blocks that allow you to change the *direction* of your sprite for just that sort of mishap. The *point in direction (__)* motion block will allow you to change the angle of the sprite's rotation. You can even make Llama turn upside down if you'd like to!

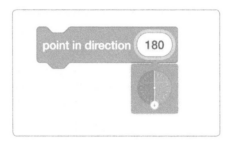

So what if you *don't* want Llama to stand on his head? Maybe you just want him to turn and face in the other direction—maybe so he can talk to another sprite who is sneaking up behind him. If you want to do that, you will need to set his rotation style before using the *point in direction (__)* motion block.

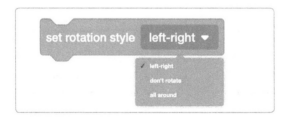

If you want Llama to face the left or the right without flipping upside down, choose the *left-right* rotation style. The next option in the drop-down menu, "don't rotate," means just that—Llama won't turn at all, no matter what kind of code is placed on him. The last option, *all around*, will let him rotate a full 360 degrees. Try them all out yourself!

# Putting It All Together

## Activity 1—Your First Script

Let's make this Llama move!

The very first thing we need for *every* program is an **event block**, or a trigger, to tell the computer to start following our directions. In Scratch, you can use the green flag to start your scripts. When you click the green flag icon above the stage, it will tell your computer to start following the list of directions in that script.

---

### STEP 1

Go to Events in your code menu. Find the *when flag clicked* event block. Click and drag the block into your script editor.

---

### STEP 2

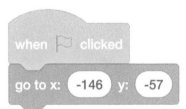

Before Llama can move, we need to tell him where to *start*. Use your mouse to drag Llama into the bottom-left corner of your stage. Then go to the Motion section in your code menu. Remember that this code will update with the coordinates of the spot you just placed Llama in, so now you just need to drag a *go to x: (__) y: (__)* motion block into your script editor. Connect it to your *when flag clicked* event block.

Now try dragging Llama with your mouse and placing him somewhere else on the stage. Click the green flag above the stage. He should move back to the coordinates you placed in your code. Go ahead—try it a few times. No matter where you move Llama, he should pop right back to the spot you programmed. Nice!

---

## STEP 3

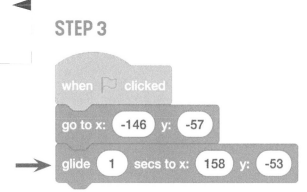

Now you have a starting position, but you still need to make Llama move to a *new* location. First, click on Llama with your mouse and move him to the bottom-right corner of the screen. The coordinates in your motion block will update to his new position. Then go to the Motion section in your code menu. Drag in a *glide (__) secs to x: (__) y: (__)* motion block and connect it to your script. The preset amount of time will be one second. And remember, the coordinates will already be loaded for you!

Click the flag, and Llama should move from left to right.

## STEP 4

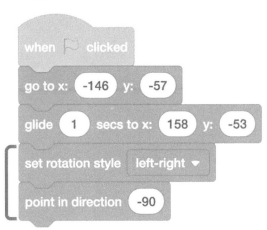

when ⚑ clicked

go to x: -146 y: -57

glide 1 secs to x: 158 y: -53

set rotation style left-right ▼

point in direction -90

Let's make Llama turn around to face the other direction. Go to Motion in your code menu. Drag in a *set rotation style (left-right)* motion block. This will change his rotation style so that if we turn him, he will face the opposite direction instead of spinning onto his head.

Next, add a *point in direction (__)* motion block. The preset value is 90 degrees, which will make Llama continue to face forward. To make him face the opposite direction, change the number to -90.

Click your flag and play your program at least twice.

Hmmm, is Llama pointing the wrong direction now at the *beginning* of the program? Yep.

Remember, our computer gets *very* confused unless we tell it every single little thing we want it to do. We programmed Llama to make a change in the direction he faces, but we forgot to tell the computer what direction Llama should face in the *beginning* of the program. This is a very common mistake that early coders make.

## STEP 5

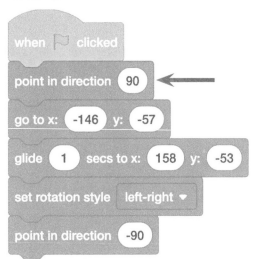

To fix the mistake, you need to add a *point in direction (90)* motion block right under your *when flag clicked* event block.

Click your flag and watch what happens. Llama should now face toward the right-hand side of the screen as he moves to the right and then flip around to face the other direction. Yay!

## STEP 6

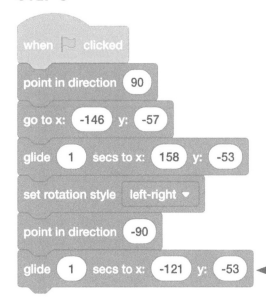

Now can you make him go back to the side he started from?

Click on Llama and place him on the left side of the screen. Then drag in another *glide (__) secs to x: (__) y: (__)* motion block, and connect it to your script. Now Llama should glide to the new position.

You just wrote your first script! Way to go! I *knew* you could do it.

# Activity 2—Go, Llama, Go!

Now let's practice other ways to move Llama around!

---

## STEP 1

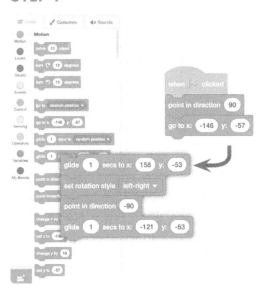

First, pull the bottom four code blocks off your script and leave them sitting there. All that should still be connected to your *when flag clicked* event block is the *point in direction 90* motion block and the *go to x: (__) y: (__)* motion block.

The code blocks you pulled off won't affect your program because they are not attached to an event block anymore. Without an event block, the code does nothing. You can leave this extra code off to the side in your script editor, or you can delete it. To delete it, drag it on top of your code menu on the left. Hover above the code menu and then let go. *Poof!* It should disappear.

## STEP 2

```
when [flag] clicked
point in direction 90
go to x: -146 y: -57
change x by 100
change y by 100
```

Now add a *change x by (__)* motion block to your script. This code block is preset to the number 10. This means that the sprite will move 10 spots to the right on the x-axis. That's a very tiny movement for a sprite, and it will be hard to notice, so let's change that number to 100. Then add a *change y by (__)* motion block to your script, and change that number to 100, too. Now you're telling the sprite to move right on the x-axis by 100 and then up on the y-axis by 100.

Click your flag. See how Llama pops up in a new spot? We don't see him move right on the x-axis and then up on the y-axis. Click your flag again, and Llama won't move at all. He just seems stuck in one spot. What's going on here?

Well, with the *glide (__) secs to x: (__) y: (__)* motion blocks that we used before, Llama was programmed to spend one second moving to the new set of coordinates so we could see it happen. That was the "glide 1 secs" part of the command.

With the code we have *now,* there are no timing instructions for the computer to follow. This means the computer moves so quickly through the list of directions that we don't even see anything happening. To us, Llama just instantly appears at his ending spot!

## STEP 3

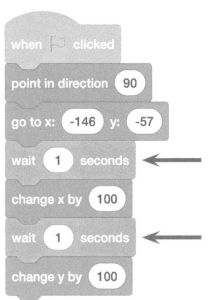

Let's add some timing so we can see Llama's movements. To do this, you need to use a control block. Go to Control in your code menu and drag out two *wait (\_\_) seconds* control blocks. They will already have a 1 in the box, which means the computer will wait one second before moving to the next code block on the list. Place one *wait (1) seconds* control block after your starting coordinates (go to x) and the second *wait (1) seconds* control block after the change in the x-coordinate (change x by 100), just like in the picture.

Now click the flag. Llama should visibly move forward and then move up. Now, can you make him turn to face the left side? And then add code to make him move back to the left side of the stage?

You can do it—give it a try! One of the most important things about coding is being willing to experiment and try different ways of doing things. If your first idea doesn't work, make some changes and try again!

## STEP 4: CODE COMPLETE!

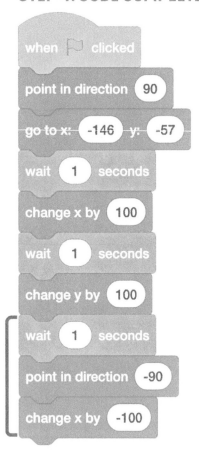

when ⚑ clicked

point in direction 90

go to x: -146 y: -57

wait 1 seconds

change x by 100

wait 1 seconds

change y by 100

wait 1 seconds

point in direction -90

change x by -100

I bet you got Llama moving with no problem! But if you're still not quite sure, here's one possible solution. First add a *wait (1) seconds* control block. Then add a *point in direction ( )* motion block and change the number to -90. Then add a *change x by ( )* motion block. To make Llama move to the left, you need to use a *negative* number. In this case, -100 will put him right back to the far left of the screen!

There are other ways to move your sprite around, but *glide ( ) secs to x: ( ) y: ( )*, *change x by ( )*, and *change y by ( )* motion blocks are the most useful. Practice using this type of code to move Llama all around.

# Hacker Hints

**1** Not sure what a code block will do to your sprite? Just click on it and see! You can preview any command by clicking on the block in the code menu list without actually adding it to your script.

And just as a note for later: If you have multiple scripts in a program, you can also click on one of them to test just that piece of the program. That's way quicker than running your entire program, especially when you are looking for bugs!

**2** Since you can move your sprite around the stage with your mouse, you might forget that you haven't actually *programmed* your sprite to be in a particular spot until you drag in a motion block and attach it to a script. Your program might seem fine the first time you run it, but if you click your flag a *second time*, your sprite might just stay there, stuck at the only coordinates you actually placed in your code. Oops! If this happens, go back into your script and give your sprite some *starting* coordinates.

# 4

# Making It Fun

In this chapter, you will learn how to make the games and programs you create in Scratch really pop! Scratch is meant to be fun, so let's check out some options that let you change sprite costumes, add backdrops, and bring in sounds. Once you know how to bring in these elements, your programs will really come alive!

## Changing Costumes

Did you know that sprites have different costumes? When you hear the word "costume," you're probably just thinking about different outfits. But in Scratch, a costume can also mean a different body position. To see a sprite's costumes, just click on the Costumes tab above your code menu.

Check out this bear! She has a costume that shows her on all fours, and she has another costume where she rises up onto her hind legs. The bear can switch between these costume options in your script.

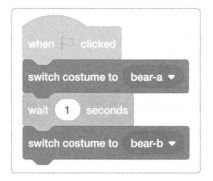

To get back to the bear's script editor, you have to click on the Code tab. It is just to the left of her Costumes tab. Then you can use a *switch costume to (__)* looks block to program the bear to start on all fours, wait one second, and then stand up. Remember, we need waits so that we actually see a change happen. Otherwise, the computer would move so quickly that all we would see is the *last* costume we chose.

If you go back to the Costumes tab, you can also make your own changes to the costumes. On the next page, we used the "bear-b" costume and selected her right arm. We can rotate it around to make her look like she's waving.

There are also drawing tools that let you add onto the picture of the bear or erase parts of it. You can even change the bear's color! You can find these tools to the left of the picture of your sprite costume when you're in the Costumes tab. You can change *any* sprite's costume; the only limit is what you can dream up!

If you click on the blue cat icon under the bear's list of costumes, a pop-up menu will appear. There are lots of different costume options. You can:

**Choose a Costume:** This will bring up the sprite library, and you can add a sprite as a new *costume*. This is useful if you want your bear to transform into something else, like a frog! It will still be the same sprite, but she will look *very* different.

**Paint:** This will create a blank costume where you can draw whatever you want.

**Surprise:** Click this if you want the program to pick a random sprite costume for you!

**Upload Costume:** You can put any picture into the Scratch program to create a costume.

**Camera:** You can click here to take a picture of yourself. It will instantly become a costume!

We've been talking about costumes, but guess what? You have these same options when it comes to adding sprites, too! For example, if you want to upload a photo to make a new sprite, just click on the same blue cat icon that appears under your stage and choose Upload Sprite.

# Choosing a Backdrop

Backdrops are like costume changes for your stage! Instead of just a plain white background, wouldn't it be more fun to choose a castle, a soccer field, or an outer space background? Just click on the backdrop icon on the very bottom right of your screen, right under where it says "Stage."

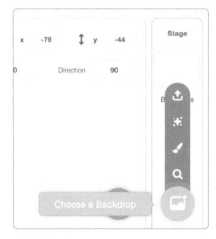

This will pull up the backdrop library, which is loaded with lots of options. Check out all the places your sprites can visit!

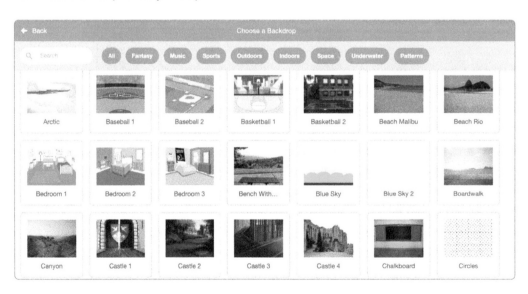

Just like with your sprites and costumes, you also have options such as drawing a backdrop or uploading your own picture to make a backdrop.

You change backdrops much like you change costumes. Just use a *switch backdrop to (\_\_)* looks block.

In the code here, we're telling the computer to show the Colorful City backdrop for five seconds and then switch to the Concert backdrop.

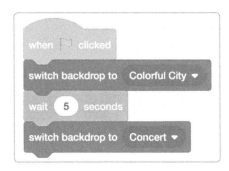

# Sound Effects

Imagine what a movie would be like without a soundtrack or sound effects. Not nearly as fun, right? Luckily, you get to be your own director when you are coding, and you're only limited by what you can think up. You can have music playing through your whole program or just use some one-time sound effects or even both!

Sometimes you might only want to add a sound once. Imagine you want a duck to make a "quacking" sound and *then* jump into a pond. That means the computer needs to wait for the quacking sound to finish *before* moving on to the next code block in the script. To do that, use a *play sound (\_\_) until done* sound block.

Other times you may want to use a continuous sound. For example, maybe you want scary music to play as a ghost starts to creep up on the duck. This means the computer should start the sound and let it continue to play as the program moves through the rest of your script. In that case, use a *start sound (\_\_)* sound block.

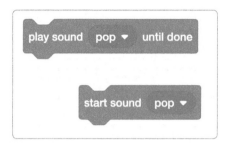

Notice that the preset sound in your code is "pop." You just need to click on the little arrow to choose other sounds. However, this part is a little tricky. Before a new sound will be available to you on the code block drop-down menu, *first* you must choose it from the sound library.

To get to the library, click on the Sounds tab above your code menu. It is right next to the Costumes tab. Then click on the sound icon on the bottom left of the screen to bring up the sound library.

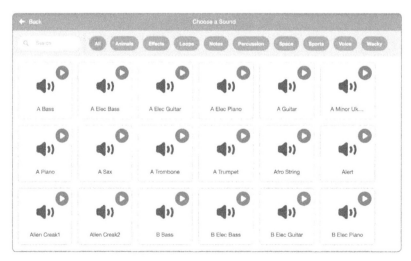

Once you have picked a sound from the sound library, it will load into your Sounds tab. Click back to the Sounds tab, and your selections will be listed just like how your sprite costumes are listed.

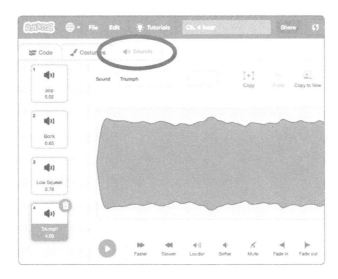

When you choose a new sound from your sound block, you will also see that "Record" is listed as an option in the drop-down menu. That means that you can record your own voice and sounds for your sprites! *Sweet!* The new recording will appear in your Sounds tab, just like any sounds you have loaded from the sound library.

## Using Libraries

Each time you added a new sprite, costume, backdrop, or sound, you visited a Scratch library. The libraries are where preloaded content is stored for you. Before any of these things can be in your program, you have to *choose* them from the library. You can get into the libraries by clicking an icon on the bottom of the screen, like the cat or backdrop icon.

# Making It Move

## Activity—Home Run Hitter

Let's use your new skills to help a baseball player hit the ball across the field! We'll combine what we've learned about costumes, backdrops, and sound tools to get really creative.

---

**4**

### STEP 1

Start by creating a brand-new program and bringing in Batter and Baseball from your sprite library. Then bring in the Baseball 2 backdrop from the backdrop library. Position the batter so that she is standing next to home plate. Place the baseball on the far left of the screen, like it has just been pitched and is heading toward her.

---

### STEP 2

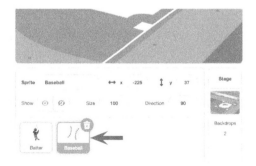

Let's start with the code for your baseball. Click on the little thumbnail image of the baseball underneath the stage to bring up its script editor. Notice that there is now a baseball icon in the script editor as well. This means that any code you place is affecting *that* sprite.

## STEP 3

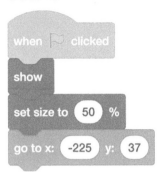

You need a *when flag clicked* event block to start your script. Add a *show* looks block to tell the computer to make your baseball visible. You may be thinking, *But my baseball is already visible!* You're right, sprites always start out visible. But if we plan on *hiding* them at any point in the program, we need to show them at the beginning, or they'll stay hidden when you restart the program.

Have you noticed that the baseball looks HUGE? Let's fix that by adding a *set size to (__) %* looks block. It's preset to 100%, but you can change that to 50%. Then add a *go to x: (__) y: (__)* motion block to choose the baseball's start position.

Click your green flag, and your baseball should shrink down to a more realistic size. Much better!

4

## STEP 4

```
when [flag] clicked
show
set size to 50 %
go to x: -225 y: 37
glide 1 secs to x: 56 y: 55
glide 1 secs to x: -231 y: 145
hide
```

4

Now use your mouse to drag your baseball over to your batter. Place it a little bit in front of the bat, leaving some room for the bat to swing forward.

Then add your *glide (__) secs to x: (__) y: (__)* motion block. Click on your baseball again and move it to the far left of the screen, like your batter has just hit a home run.

Add another *glide (__) secs to x: (__) y: (__)* motion block. Finally, add a *hide* looks block so the baseball will disappear. That will make it look like the ball has flown off into the distance! (That's why we had to make sure to "show" our baseball in the beginning of its script.)

# STEP 5

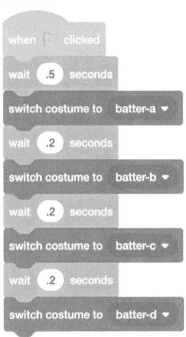

**Now click on the thumbnail of your batter.** This switches to her script editor. Click the Costumes tab above the code menu to see your options. Each of your batter's costumes shows a different part of the motion needed to swing a bat. If you program her to quickly change costumes, it looks like she is swinging her bat!

Start her script with a *when flag clicked* event block. Add a *wait (__) seconds* control block and change the timing to 0.5 seconds. You want enough time so that the ball has started to move toward her, but she still brings her bat up before the ball arrives. Then add a *switch costume to (__)* looks block for each of her four costume options. You need a *wait (__) seconds* control block between each costume change so you can see her switch through the positions, but those changes still need to happen quickly, so use a small number, like 0.2 seconds.

Experiment with your code and see how it goes. If the timing feels off, then try changing how long your waits are or adjusting the coordinates in your motion block. You've got this!

4

## STEP 6: CODE COMPLETE!

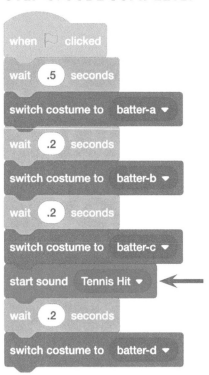

Now that our batter can hit the ball, let's add a satisfying "crack" sound effect when her bat touches the ball! Remember, first click on the Sounds tab above the code menu. Then click the sound icon on the bottom left to bring up the sound library. There are lots of options you could use, but we used "Tennis Hit." The sounds are listed alphabetically, or you can use the search bar to find the sound you want.

Once your sound effect is loaded, click the Code tab above the code menu to bring up your batter's script editor again. You can add a *start sound (__)* sound block to your existing script and choose "Tennis Hit" from its drop-down menu. Place it right after the batter switches to the batter-c costume. That's when she has the bat extended and should be making contact with the ball. *Crack!*

Awesome job! Now you know how to make a sprite move, and you know how to combine all of the Scratch elements to make up a fun game: costumes, backdrops, and sounds! In the next few chapters, you'll be able to take what you've learned about Scratch and combine it with the coding tools we talked about earlier—loops, variables, conditions, and more. You're ready to build some pretty cool code.

# Hacker Hints

**1** Want to make changes to a sprite costume without losing the original costume? Try duplicating! Just right-click on one of your sprite's costumes, and a pop-up box will appear with the option to "Duplicate" the costume. (If you're using a computer system without a right-click option on the mouse, try holding down the control key while you click on the costume. If you are using a touchpad on a laptop, try using a two-finger click on the costume.)

**2** We chose a baseball backdrop for our batter, but we didn't actually place any code with it. If we had wanted the backdrop to *change* during our program, we would have needed to put the backdrops into our code. Here's an example of what it would look like if we wanted the sprite to start in a baseball field and then switch to a basketball court.

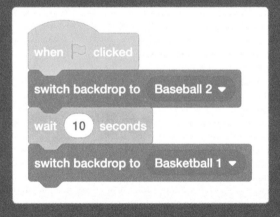

# 5

# Loops

Imagine you are making a necklace with a specific pattern. You could string each bead one by one—red, blue, green, purple, and so on—but that would take a long time! Or you could design a super cool *loop machine* that places each bead in the correct order every time!

In coding, loops are how we create repetition. A loop is code that you place around *other* pieces of code to make that code repeat itself over and over.

Let's say you want to change the bead pattern on your imaginary necklace. That's fine—the loop machine makes it easy. Just program a new pattern into the machine, and the power of loops can make 1 necklace, 10 necklaces, or even 100 necklaces in no time.

In coding, using loops to repeat the same set of directions saves you time and work. Loops also reduce the chances of making a mistake because you'll know for sure the directions are being repeated *exactly*.

# Loops in Scratch

Now that you know what loops are, let's see how we can use them in Scratch!

## Activity 1—Taco Time

I know a dog who *really* loves tacos. Let's use a loop to help him get one!

### STEP 1

Bring in Dog2 sprite and Taco sprite, placing them on opposite sides of the stage.

## STEP 2

The taco is so enormous, it looks like *it* could eat the dog instead of the other way around! Let's make it smaller. On the taco script editor, drag in a *when flag clicked* event block and a *set size (__) %* looks block. Type in the number 50, and now the taco will be half as big. Next, add a *show* looks block so the computer knows that the taco should be visible at the start of the program. This matters now because we will want the taco to hide after it's eaten by the dog.

## STEP 3

**Go to the script editor for the dog.** Drag in a *when flag clicked* event block and use a *go to x: (__) y: (__)* motion block to set his start position.

## STEP 4

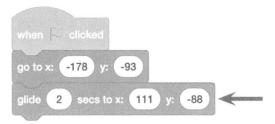

Go to your stage and drag the dog over until he is barely touching the taco. Add a *glide (__) secs to x: (__) y: (__)* motion block to your script. Change the amount of time for the glide to 2 seconds.

Click the flag to test what you have so far. The dog should start on the left side and then glide to the taco.

## STEP 5

```
when [flag] clicked

go to x: -178 y: -93

glide 2 secs to x: 111 y: -88

switch costume to dog2-a ▼

wait .2 seconds

switch costume to dog2-b ▼
```

Now let's use some costume changes to make the dog's feet move while he glides. Add a *switch costume to (__)* looks block and make sure "dog2-a" is selected from the drop-down menu. Then place a *wait (__) seconds* control block. Change the amount of time to something very small, like 0.2 seconds, so the costume changes quickly. Next, add another *switch costume to (__)* looks block, and this time select "dog2-b" from the drop-down menu.

Run your program and watch what happens.

Hmmm. Not quite what we wanted, is it? The dog glides to the taco, and *then* he moves his feet. We want him to move his feet *while* he glides.

Remember that your computer only does one thing at a time, and it follows your directions in exact order. Right now, you are telling it to complete the glide command *before* completing the costume change. If you want the costume changes to happen at the same time as the gliding, then you need to create a separate list of code with the same event block, so when you click the flag, both sets of code will be followed at the same time.

## STEP 6

Drag out a brand-new *when flag clicked* event block. Then unhook your costume-changing code from your original script and attach it to the new event. Now when you run the program, the computer will follow the directions for both lists at the exact same time. Each list is a script, so in this program you now have *two* scripts!

---

## STEP 7

Right now, the dog moves his feet, but he only moves them once—he doesn't do it the whole time he is gliding toward the taco. Instead of adding more costume code, we can use a loop! First, add on one more *wait (__) seconds* control block to your script, and change the amount of time to 0.2 seconds. Remember, we need the pause before the next costume change so we actually see it happening. Then drag out a *repeat* control block and place it *just* around all of the costume-changing code. That's your loop! Try changing the number of repeats to 4. If that isn't quite right, adjust the number of repeats until you find the number that works best for your program. Now he should be walking right up to that taco. Good job using that loop to get him there!

5

## STEP 8: CODE COMPLETE!

Once the dog reaches the taco, we want to make the taco disappear so that it looks like the dog gobbled it up! **To do this, go back to the taco's script editor by clicking the taco icon under the stage.** You'll see the code you already placed to make the taco smaller and to make it visible.

Since it takes some time for the dog to glide to the taco, let's add a *wait (__) seconds* control block at the bottom of your taco script so it disappears at just the right moment. You need to change the time for the wait to two seconds because that is how long it takes for the dog to get to the taco. Then add a *hide* looks block. See? The taco disappears after the dog touches it.

5

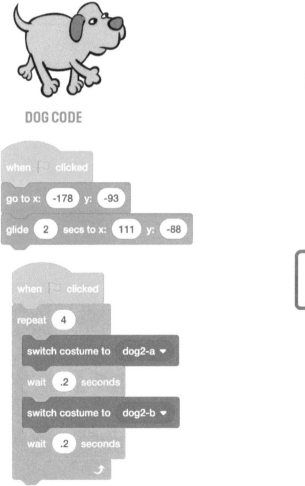

DOG CODE

TACO CODE

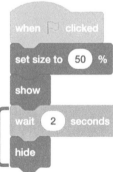

## YOUR TURN!

Now that you've coded this activity, try challenging yourself to make the following changes:

☐  Make the dog glide faster.

☐  Add another sprite for the dog to eat.

☐  Add a "chomp" sound effect whenever the dog eats something!

5

# Activity 2—Dance Party

Now that you have some experience with loops, let's use some to throw a dance party! Good thing Scratch has awesome dancers!

---

## STEP 1

Find Ben and Max in your sprites library and load them into a new program.

---

## STEP 2

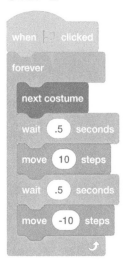

**Go to Ben's script editor.** Since *all* of Ben's costumes involve different dance positions, we can use a *next costume* looks block. Remember to add a *wait (__) seconds* control block so there is a pause before he switches costumes. Choose a small number, such as 0.5 seconds, so he will switch costumes pretty quickly. Then give him a little side-to-side movement. Try using a *move 10 steps* motion block, adding a *wait (__) seconds* control block, and then finishing with a *move -10 steps* motion block. Then wrap that *forever* control block around everything. Check out his moves!

## STEP 3

**Now switch to Max's script editor.** Take a look at Max's costumes under the Costumes tab. Notice how the fourth costume, max-d, shows her holding a basketball. You don't want a basketball randomly appearing and disappearing while Max dances—that would be super weird!

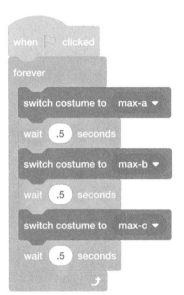

Begin a new script with a *when flag clicked* event block. Instead of using the *next costume* shortcut, you need to choose the exact costumes you want to use—max-a, max-b, and max-c—so go ahead and drag over three *switch costume to (__)* looks blocks. Don't forget your *wait (__) seconds* control block between each change. You can still use a *forever* control block to make her repeat the costume changes. Try it out and shorten the wait time to 0.5 seconds to make her dance faster.

## STEP 4

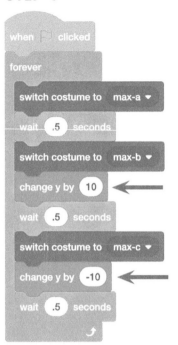

Let's make Max jump when she throws up her arms! Jumping means that she will be moving up and down on the y-axis. Use a *change y by 10* motion block to make her jump up when she is wearing the max-a costume, and use a *change y by -10* motion block to make her land back on the ground when she is wearing the max-c costume.

## STEP 5

It's not a dance party without a fun backdrop! Try loading the Party backdrop from your Scratch library.

## STEP 6: CODE COMPLETE!

Hmmm, something is missing. What could it be?

Music! Pick out a fun song from the Scratch sound library. How about "Dance Celebrate"?

You could add your sound code to either of your sprites, but let's go ahead and place it on Max. Place a *start sound (__)* sound block right under her *when flag clicked* event block. Click the arrow to select your song.

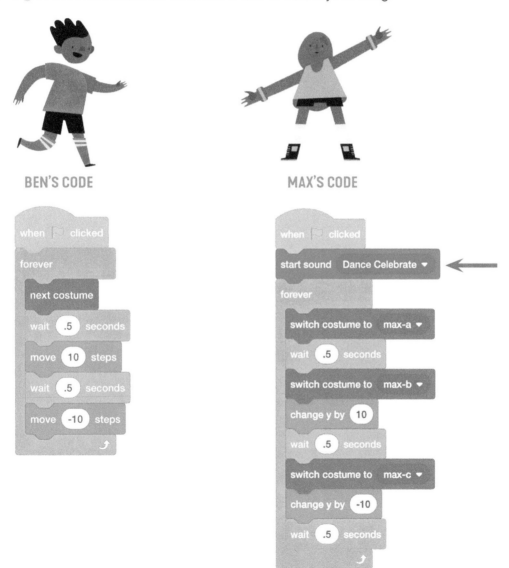

BEN'S CODE                                    MAX'S CODE

## YOUR TURN!

Now that you've coded this activity, try challenging yourself to make the following changes:

☐ Use *turn* motion code to give your dancers more movement.

☐ Add some more backdrops and then use a loop to make them switch out during the dance party.

☐ Use a *say* looks code block to make Ben and Max talk! What funny things can you make them say?

5

# Activity 3—Dodge the Stars

Ripley the astronaut has to watch out for falling stars when he's flying through space. Can you use some loops to help him out?

---

## STEP 1

Bring in the Ripley sprite and center him on the bottom of the stage. Then bring in the Star sprite three times so that you get three different star sprites. (You can also do this by right-clicking the star icon and choosing *duplicate*.) Arrange them in a row across the top of the stage.

5

---

## STEP 2

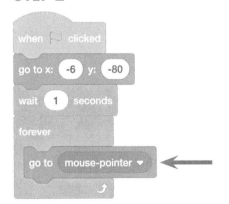

**Go to Ripley's script editor.** Start the script with a *when flag clicked* event block, and then add a *go to x: (__) y: (__)* motion block to set his start position. Add a *wait (1) seconds* control block.

We can do something really cool now—we can make Ripley follow our mouse *wherever* it goes! All you need to do is add a *forever* control block and place a *go to (random position)* motion block inside it. But instead of going to random positions, click the little arrow in the motion block to choose "mouse-pointer."

Now try running your script. Experiment with taking out the *wait (1) seconds* control block. See how Ripley gets stuck in the top-left corner at first? That's because the program starts the instant you click the flag. And where is your mouse when you click the flag? Yep, that's why Ripley pops up in that corner! Using the wait gives a smoother start to your game.

---

## STEP 3

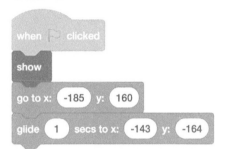

5

**Go to the first star's script editor.** Start your script with a *when flag clicked* event block, add a *show* looks block to make it visible, and then add a *go to x: (__) y: (__)* motion block to give it a starting point. To make the star actually fall, click and drag the star straight down until it's at the bottom of the screen. That will update your motion code blocks with the new coordinates. Then add a *glide (__) secs to x: (__) y: (__)* motion block to your script.

## STEP 4

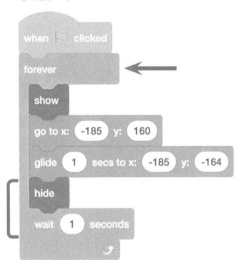

To make the star look like it has fallen *past* Ripley, add a *hide* looks block. Then add a *wait (__) seconds* control block. Finally, place all of the code inside a *forever* control block so that it will constantly repeat. That wait we added helps make it look like it's a *new* star falling from the top of the screen. Without the wait, it looks like the same star is just jumping back up to the top of the screen.

## STEP 5

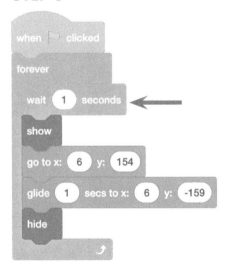

**Go to Star2's script editor.** You can build your code for Star2 the exact same way, with one small adjustment. Since Star2 is right above Ripley's head, move the *wait (__) seconds* control block to the top of the script instead of the bottom. That way, the user has enough time to move Ripley out of the way before the star begins to fall. This will also change the timing for Star2 so it feels more random. Otherwise, it will fall down right next to the first star. If all three stars fall down in a straight line, Ripley never gets a chance to dodge them!

## STEP 6: CODE COMPLETE!

Can you figure out how to code your last star? Try following the same strategy we used for the other stars, but this time change the *wait (__) seconds* control block to two seconds so Star3 will have different timing from the other two. This should make the falling stars feel more random.

If you're quick with your mouse, you can make Ripley an expert star dodger!

**RIPLEY'S CODE**  **STAR CODE**  **STAR2 CODE**  **STAR3 CODE**

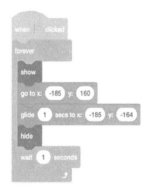
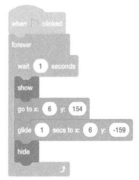
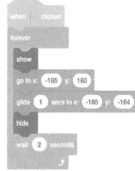

## YOUR TURN!

Now that you've coded this activity, try challenging yourself to make the following changes:

☐ Adjust your waits to make the star movements even more random.

☐ Add more sprites for Ripley to dodge.

☐ Make one of the new sprites shoot across the stage from left to right instead of falling from the top of the screen.

# Loops Off-Screen

Did you know that you use loops all the time in your normal daily life? Think about it! You're constantly doing things over and over without thinking about every little step. For example, think about when you are eating popcorn at the movie theater. If you were a computer, you would use the following directions: Pick up a piece of popcorn, place in your mouth, chew, swallow. And repeat!

# Exploring More!

Loops are great for saving you time and making your code much shorter. But they are also really important for setting up situations where the computer can always check for a certain condition, or rule, that you make. For example, if you create a rule that you should score a point every time the ball sprite goes into the basket, then you will need a *forever* control block around that code to tell the computer to constantly check for that condition.

It's a good thing you understand loops now because we will need them in our next chapter, when we learn how to use variables!

# Hacker Hints

**1** If you have sprites that need similar code, just duplicate the code and make small changes instead of dragging in new code. To duplicate a script, right-click on the code and choose *Duplicate*. Duplicating code can be a good starting point, but you'll also need to make some adjustments. For example, if you had duplicated the code from Star for Star2 and Star3, then you would have needed to adjust the coordinates in all the motion blocks for the new stars.

**2** What if you've done a bunch of work coding a bear to chase your cat sprite, when suddenly you realize it would be *way better* if the cat were being chased by a fire-breathing dragon instead? If you delete the bear, you lose all of that great code you wrote! Here's what you can do: Go ahead and bring in that dragon. Then click on the code you have for your bear and drag it on top of the new dragon sprite icon underneath the stage. Just hover the code over the dragon and release. Go to your dragon script editor, and there should now be a copy of all your code. Then delete your bear. You just switched out sprites without losing any of your code!

# Coder's Checklist

You learned lots of useful things in this chapter, including how to:

☐ Use a loop to repeat a sequence of directions

☐ Use a loop to make a sprite follow your mouse

☐ Use a loop to create a visual illusion

☐ Use the next costume shortcut

☐ Run multiple scripts at once

If any of these feel a little unclear, you can always flip back and read this chapter again.

5

# 6

# Variables

A variable is a place to store something. Think of it as a box that can hold just one thing at a time. For example, you could have a box to hold candy. First, you might put a chocolate in the box. Your variable *name* would be candy. Your variable *value* would be chocolate. You can take the chocolate out and put in a caramel instead. Your variable name has not changed—it is still candy. But now your variable value has changed to caramel. You would express this information as *candy = caramel*.

In coding, that box stores information. You open up the box, or variable, to get to the information when you need it in your program.

There are different types of variables:

One type of variable is called a **string**. A string means that the information you are storing is a group of different characters. It could be a combination of letters, numbers, or other symbols. It could be the word "basketball." Basically, a string is anything you might type using your computer keyboard.

Another type of variable is a **number**. In Scratch, numbers can be whole numbers or decimals. The clock that counts down the time during a sports game is a variable. When there are 10 seconds left on the clock, you would say that your timer = 10. When there are nine seconds left on the clock, you would say your timer = 9. You might also say, "Hurry up and score that basket!"

Scratch also uses **Booleans**. These are variables that only have two possible values: true or false. Booleans help you make rules, or conditions, in your program. For example, you could make a rule that if your sprite goes out of bounds, it loses a point. Or you could make a rule that if your score equals 10, your sprite can move on to the next level.

# Variables in Scratch

Now that you know what variables are, let's see how we can use them in Scratch!

## Activity 1—Talk to a Sprite!

LEVEL UP!

Let's learn how to use a variable to talk to our sprites. Abby would love to meet you!

-------------------------------------------------------------------

**STEP 1**

Select Abby from your sprite library.

-------------------------------------------------------------------

**STEP 2**

Start your new script for Abby by placing a *when flag clicked* event block and an *ask ( ) and wait* sensing block. There is already a question in the block: "What's your name?" You can stick with that for now. Click the flag to run your program. You will notice that Abby asks you the question, and a box pops up in the bottom of the screen for you to type in your answer. After you type a response, click the checkmark to the right of the box or just hit return on your keyboard. Whatever you type into that box will be stored in the *answer* sensing block. This code block is also a variable since it is storing information for us.

---

## STEP 3

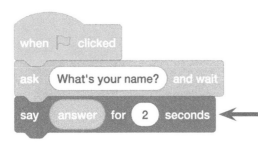

To make Abby respond to us, add a *say (__) for 2 seconds* looks block. The code block says "Hello," but you can type over it to make the sprite say anything you want. In this case, drag your *answer* sensing block *into* the text bubble. It may take some practice, but you want to hover the *answer* sensing block over the text bubble and then release it to allow it to snap into place. Run your program and type your own name when Abby asks for it. Abby should repeat your name back because you stored it in your answer **variable**. Pretty cool, huh? Try typing something else. It can even be a whole phrase, like "Monkeys love bananas!" Abby will repeat it back to you.

## STEP 4: CODE COMPLETE!

Let's make it more interesting. Add another *say (__) for 2 seconds* looks block and type "is a great name!" in the text bubble.

Now Abby should tell you that you have a great name! Thanks, Abby!

---

## YOUR TURN!

Now that you've coded this activity, try challenging yourself to make the following changes:

☐ Program Abby to ask another question.

☐ Add movement and costume changes to make Abby more animated while she talks to you.

☐ Use the answer sensing block to program Abby to give a funny response.

# Activity 2—Riddle Me This!

Now that you've been properly introduced, Abby would love to tell you a riddle, but she doesn't have all day. Can you answer her riddle in under 10 seconds?

We can use a variable to make a timer that can count down the seconds. This time, you will be creating your own *unique* variable. How cool is that?

First, let's get rid of the code we already have and start fresh. Just drag all of Abby's code back to your code menu and release it to delete it.

--------------------------------------------------------------------------------

## STEP 1

**Variables**

Make a Variable

**New Variable** ✕

New variable name:

| Timer |

◉ For all sprites  ○ For this sprite only

Cancel  **OK**

**Variables**

Make a Variable

☐ my variable

☑ Timer

Go to the Variables section on your code menu and click on the *Make a Variable* button at the top of the list. In the pop-up box, type the name *Timer*. Then click OK. You will see that your new variable is now listed as an option in your variable code block list.

When you clicked on your variable code list, you may have noticed there is already something called *my variable* in the list. This is a general variable that we could have used. But it's usually a good idea to name any new variable that you create. This helps you stay organized, especially if you will be creating lots of variables. Also, in this case, you want the text for your variable (timer) to display on your game screen. It wouldn't make much sense if it said, "my variable" on the screen instead of "Timer," right?

## STEP 2

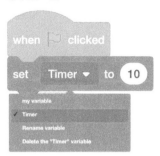

Next, we need to tell the program what value your variable should have when the program begins. To begin your script, drag in a *when flag clicked* event block and then add a *set my variable to (__)* variable block. You'll need to make some adjustments to this new code block. First, click the down arrow to select the *"Timer"* variable you just made. Then change the number from 0 to 10. This gives your timer variable a starting value of 10 seconds.

## STEP 3

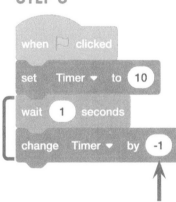

Now we have a timer, but how do we make it count down? First, add a *wait (__) seconds* control block. By default, the wait will have a 1 in the text box. That's perfect! A timer counts down after every second, right? Then add a *change my variable by (1)* variable block. You'll need to make some adjustments to this variable code block. First, click the down arrow to select Timer, the variable you created. Then change the number value from 1 to -1. Changing the timer by -1 means that the value of the variable will go down by one whole number. Now your timer should change from 10 to 9 after the one-second wait.

## STEP 4

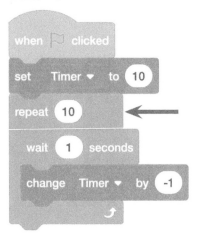

Now put a *repeat* control block just around the last two code blocks so that your timer will count down to zero. How many times should it repeat so that we end on zero? Ten!

---

## STEP 5

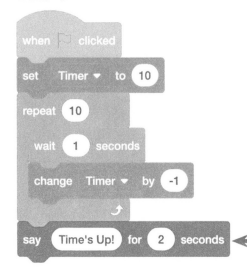

Add a *say (__) for 2 seconds* looks block to make Abby announce, "Time's up!" Make sure you place this code block *after* the repeat loop so the countdown is what's looping, not Abby's announcement.

If we had included the *say (__) for 2 seconds* code inside of the repeat loop, she would have said "Time's Up!" after every single second. We don't want that!

## STEP 6: CODE COMPLETE!

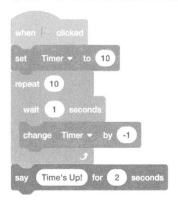

Now we have our timer, but where is the riddle? You will need to use an *ask (__) and wait* sensing block. If you want the timer to count down at the same time that you're inputting your answer, the riddle needs to be asked in a separate script. So leave the script for your timer where it is. Go ahead and drag out a brand-new *when flag clicked* event block. Then add an *ask (__) and wait* sensing block.

Ready for the riddle? Type this into your *ask (__) and wait* sensing block: *What is full of keys but never opens a door?*

Click your flag and see if you can guess the riddle in under 10 seconds! Did you get it?

The answer is a *piano*. A piano is full of keys that you press to play the music, but they are not the kind of keys that can open up a door!

---

## YOUR TURN!

Now that you've coded this activity, try challenging yourself to make the following changes:

☐ Add a buzzer sound when the timer hits zero!

☐ Give Abby a costume change after she asks her question.

☐ Try changing the timer to count *up* to 10 instead of down to zero.

# Activity 3—Sneak Past the Shark

Pufferfish sees some tasty food ahead, but she has to get past the shark to reach it! Let's use a variable to help Pufferfish sneak past the shark. With a variable, we can change a sprite's speed to go faster or slower. We can even use it to make Pufferfish stop immediately if the shark has spotted her. Just don't let her get caught, or she'll become a shark snack!

---

## STEP 1

Begin a new program with Pufferfish and Shark2 sprite. Arrange them like you see here.

---

## STEP 2

**Go to Pufferfish's script editor.** Drag in a *when flag clicked* event block and a *go to x: (\_) y: (\_)* motion block to give Pufferfish her starting point.

---

## STEP 3

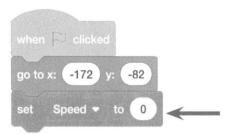

Create a brand-new variable like you did for the Timer in our last activity and name it "speed." Add a *set (speed) to (0)* variable block so Pufferfish always starts with no speed. (Remember to select your new variable from the drop-down menu in the code block.)

## STEP 4

To change Pufferfish's speed, pull out a *move (__) steps* motion block. The bigger the number of steps our sprite is taking, the faster she will appear to move. The smaller the number of steps she is taking, the slower she will appear to move.

We want Pufferfish to go faster or slower based on input from the user. That means the number of steps in the *move (__) steps* motion block needs to be changeable. To do that, drag the *speed* variable block you made into the code block.

---

## STEP 5

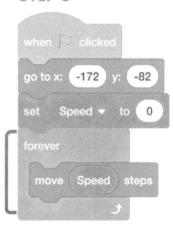

To keep Pufferfish moving constantly, add a *forever* control block around the *move (speed) steps* motion block and connect it to your script.

Run your program and see what happens. Umm, nothing, right? So far you have set your variable's value to zero, which means Pufferfish will move zero steps. Now you need to add in some events to make the value of your speed variable change.

## STEP 6

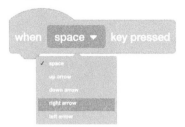

Stay in Pufferfish's script editor and start a new script with a *when (___) key pressed* event block. Click the drop-down menu to select the right-arrow key. Pushing that key will make Pufferfish move forward.

## STEP 7

To make Pufferfish speed up when we push the right-arrow key, we have to increase the value of our variable. To do this, add a *change (___) by 1* variable block. Choose "*speed*" from your drop-down menu of options.

Try it out! Notice that if you press the right-arrow key once, the speed is set at *move 1 step* and Pufferfish moves slowly forward. Tap the right-arrow key a few more times. Her speed increases because she is moving by more steps at a time.

## STEP 8

Let's add a new key to make her stop quickly when she sees the shark. Start a new script following steps 6 and 7, but *this* time change your event block to *when (down arrow) key pressed*. Then add a *set (speed) to (0)* variable block to cause Pufferfish to stop.

Now she should be able to swim faster and faster the more you push the right-arrow key, but she can also instantly stop in her tracks whenever you press the down arrow. She's a nimble little fish!

---

## STEP 9

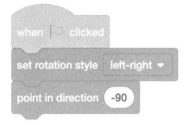

**Now switch to your shark's script editor.**
Start his script with a *when flag clicked* event. Then add a *set rotation style (left-right)* motion block and a *point in direction (-90)* motion block to make the shark face Pufferfish.

## STEP 10: CODE COMPLETE!

If the shark is always staring down at Pufferfish, she won't get much of a chance to sneak by him, will she? So let's also program our shark to disappear every once in a while. Add a *forever* control block. Inside the block, place a **show** looks block, a *wait (1) seconds* control block, a **hide** looks block, and another *wait (1) seconds* control block. The loop will keep him hiding and popping up, well, forever!

Now try out your code! Make Pufferfish stop every time the shark appears—you've made your own version of the game Red Light, Green Light!

**PUFFER FISH CODE**

**SHARK CODE**

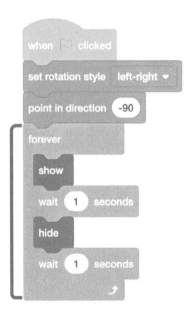

## YOUR TURN!

Now that you've coded this activity, try challenging yourself to make the following changes:

☐ Add a scary sound effect every time the shark appears.

☐ Change the timing of the wait controls to make the appearance of the shark more random.

☐ Add more movement for pufferfish. What could happen if you press the up arrow? Or the back arrow?

# Variables Off-Screen

We use variables all the time in the real world. Imagine that the days of the week are different variables and that the activities you do each day change the value of that variable. For example, on Mondays you might have piano lessons, and on Thursdays you might have soccer practice. So the variables would be Monday = piano and Thursday = soccer. See if you can spot some variables in your daily life!

# Exploring More!

Variables can do lots of cool things in your programs. You can use them to keep score, change speed, create gravity—there's really an infinite number of possibilities. If you can imagine it, you can probably do it!

Variables can also make your code much more efficient. Think about how much more code we would have needed to program Pufferfish's movements if we hadn't used a variable!

# Hacker Hints

**1** When you make a variable, *you* get to decide if you want it to be visible on the screen! Just check or uncheck the box next to your variable in your code list. But what if sometimes you want your variable to be showing in your program, and at other times you do *not* want it to be visible? Then you can use a *show variable (___)* or a *hide variable (___)* variable block to tell the computer when you want it showing on the screen.

**2** Whenever you use a variable, don't forget to set its value at the beginning of your program. Think carefully about what the value of your variable should be every time you start a program. It doesn't always need to be zero. Try testing different starting values until you find the right one.

# Coder's Checklist

You learned lots of interesting things in this chapter, including how to:

☐ Use a string variable to store user input, like when we told Abby our name on page 78

☐ Code your program to give a string variable as an output, like when we had Abby say "_____ is a great name!" on page 79

☐ Create your own variable

☐ Set and change the value of a variable

Remember, if any of these feel a little unclear, you can always flip back and reread this chapter.

# 7

# Conditions

Conditions let you create rules for your computer to follow as it works through your scripts. One tool for creating a condition is an *If . . . then statement*. You make statements like this all day long. For example, you might say, *"If* I eat all my dinner, *then* I will get dessert." You are making a rule that *eating all your dinner = getting dessert*.

You also have *If . . . then . . . else statements*. For example, *"If* it is hot outside, *then* I will go swimming. *Or else* I will go to the library." In this case, the rule is that *hot weather = going swimming* and *other types of weather = going to the library*.

Conditions let you *really* boss your computer around to create different paths for your programs to follow. These paths depend on what the user does. For example, you can make rules about what you want to happen depending on where your user clicks on the screen.

# Conditions in Scratch

Now that you've learned about conditions, let's see how we can use them in Scratch!

## Activity 1—What's the Password?

LEVEL UP!

Have you ever wanted to visit a castle? This one is closely guarded by a very strict knight. He won't let anyone near the castle gate unless they can tell him the secret password. But how will the knight know if you get the password right? We're going to use a condition to help him out.

---

**STEP 1**

Knight

Castle 1

Castle 2

Bring in Knight from your sprite library. Then load Castle1 and Castle2 from your backdrops library.

## STEP 2

On the knight's script editor page, begin your script with a *when flag clicked* event block. Then use a *switch backdrop to (__)* looks block to select Castle2 so you start with the picture of a pathway leading to a castle. Add a *show* looks block to make the knight visible.

Next, position the knight in the middle of the path so he is blocking the way to the castle. Add a *go to x: (__) y: (__)* motion block to set his position. Then use an *ask (__) and wait* sensing block to make the knight demand the password. Type, "Halt! What is the password?" in the text box.

## STEP 3

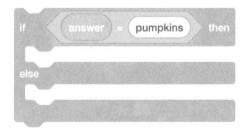

Time for your condition! These are found in the Control section of your code menu because they *control* your scripts. Drag out an *If (__) then (__) else (__)* control block. Do you notice the hexagon shape? The only kind of code block that can fit in there is an operator block. Go ahead and drag in a hexagon-shaped *(__) = (__)* operator block. Then drag an *answer* sensing block into the first oval inside the operator block. The second oval in the operator block will have the number 50. Hmmm, that is a pretty boring password, isn't it? Type in the word "pumpkins" instead.

Or choose whatever word you want! But remember, that's the password you will have to type to get the knight to let you pass to the castle gates. By the way, the operator block we just used is a type of variable called a Boolean. A Boolean can only have two possible values: true or false. In this case, the computer is asking itself: Did the user type "pumpkins"? True or false?

## STEP 4

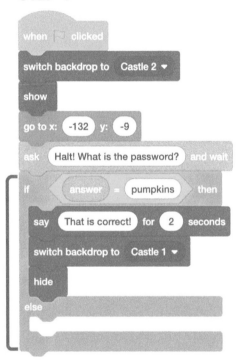

Now connect the condition you made in Step 3 to the rest of your script. So far, we have only written the first part of the rule. *If the answer is pumpkins, then . . .?* What should the knight do? Well, everything you want to happen *after* you give the correct password goes right inside the first section of the *If (__) then (__) else (__)* control block.

First, make the knight tell us that we got the right answer. Add a *say (__) for (__) seconds* looks block. Replace the preset text (Hello) with "That is correct!" Then add a *switch backdrop to (__)* looks block and choose "Castle1" from the drop-down menu so the backdrop will switch to the castle gate. Finally, use a *hide* looks block so the knight will disappear.

## STEP 5: CODE COMPLETE!

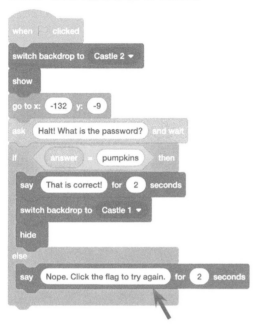

The "else" part of your control is where you tell your computer what to do if the answer given is *anything* different from the password. This is a great shortcut for us. Can you imagine trying to code every possible answer someone might type in? In this case, you just want to identify the *right* answer—anything different from that will get the same response.

Drag out a *say (__) for (__) seconds* looks block and type in, "Nope. Click the flag to try again." Place this code inside the *else* section of your condition.

Now you have a loyal knight who won't let anyone pass unless they know the secret password!

----

## YOUR TURN!

Now that you've coded this activity, try challenging yourself to make the following changes:

☐ Add to your condition so the knight leads you up the path if you get the password right.

☐ Add to your condition so the knight gets angry if you get the password wrong.

☐ Add a dragon sprite that stands next to the knight and breathes fire.

7

# Activity 2—Space Ride

Can you help an alien fly through outer space in a rocket ship? You sure can, using conditions—let's launch her!

---

## STEP 1

Bring in Rocket Ship sprite and the Stars backdrop.

---

## STEP 2

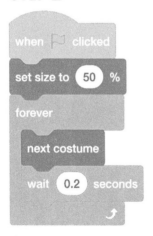

Our rocket ship is kind of big, but we know how to adjust this! Start the rocket ship's script with a *when flag clicked* event block and then add a *set size to (__) %* looks block. Change the value to 50%. Then use a *forever* control block and a *next costume* looks block with a *wait (__) seconds* control block to make the rocket ship keep changing costumes. Choose a small amount of time for the wait, like 0.2 seconds. Now the alien really looks like she's flying!

The costumes are making the rocket ship look pretty animated, but wouldn't it be way cooler to move the rocket ship forward with your right-arrow key? We can use a condition to do that!

---

## STEP 3

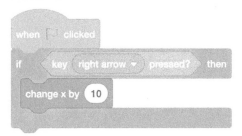

Bring in a *when flag clicked* event block to start a new script. This time you will use an *If (___) then* control block to set up your rule.

Think about the rule we are writing. Using an *If . . . then statement*, we would say, "If the user presses the right-arrow key, move the rocket ship to the right on the x-axis." To write this into your code, drag a hexagon-shaped *key (___) pressed?* sensing block and drop it into the empty hexagon of your *If (___) then* control block. Select "right-arrow" from the drop-down menu of the sensing block. Then inside the condition, place a *change x by (___)* motion block. You can leave it with the preset value of 10.

Test it out! Does the alien's rocket ship move forward when you press the right-arrow key?

Hmmm, not so much.

Let's take a minute to really think about our code. We told the computer to check for the right-arrow key being pressed, but we only told it to do that *once*. As soon as you click the green flag, the computer checks for the rule, but then it never checks again! By the time your hand flies to the arrow key, the computer has already completed its check. Remember, you have to *really* spell things out for your computer.

## STEP 4

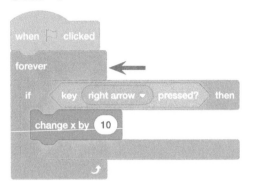

In this case, the solution is to place one of our loops, a *forever* control block, around the condition. This way, the computer knows it should *always* be checking to see if you are pressing the right-arrow key. Go ahead, add that *forever* control block and try again! Pretty awesome, right?

---

## STEP 5

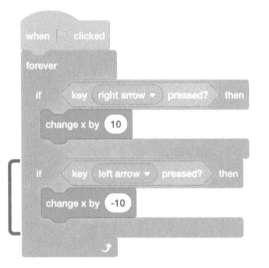

Now let's program the left-arrow key. Add another *If (___) then* control block directly after the first *If (___) then* control block. Place another *key (___) pressed?* sensing block inside it, but this time choose "left arrow" from the drop-down menu. Use a *change x by (___)* motion block again, but this time, set the value to -10 so the rocket ship will move to the *left* on the x-axis. Both of your conditions should be inside your forever loop.

7

## STEP 6: CODE COMPLETE!

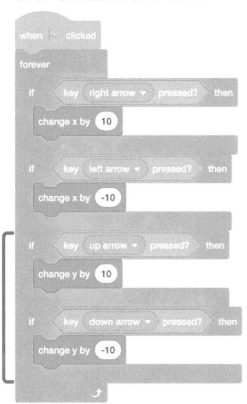

Can you make the rocket ship move up and down? To do that, it needs to move along the y-axis. Try programming the up arrow to make the rocket ship move up the y-axis and the down arrow to make the rocket ship move down the y-axis.

Good work! Now you can make the alien fly wherever you want!

7

## YOUR TURN!

Now that you've coded this activity, try challenging yourself to make the following changes:

☐ Add code to make the rocket ship turn to face in the direction it is moving whenever you press an arrow key.

☐ Add more backdrops for the alien to fly through.

☐ Add fun background music.

# Activity 3—Mission: Donuts!

Oh boy, our flying alien is about to enter an asteroid field of . . . donuts! Wow, our alien *loves* donuts. Let's help her collect as many as she can! However, if our alien collects *too* many donuts, her rocket ship will get too heavy to fly home, so we have to keep track of how many she has!

For this activity, you will be adding on to the rocket ship code we made in Activity 2—Space Ride!

---

## STEP 1

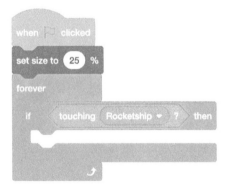

Bring in Donut sprite. On the donut's script editor, drag in a *when flag clicked* event block and then add a **set size to (__) %** looks block. Change the value to 25% so the donut will be smaller. Much better! Now, add a *forever* control block and an *If (__) then* control block.

Our new rule will be "If the rocket ship touches the donut, make the donut disappear and then reappear in a new spot." To code the first part of this rule, drag a hexagon-shaped *touching (__) ?* sensing block into the empty hexagon in your *If (__) then* control block. Choose "Rocketship" from the sensing block's drop-down menu.

7

## STEP 2

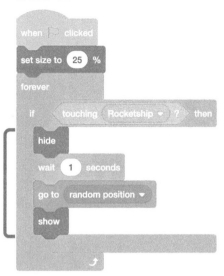

When the rocket ship makes contact with a donut, we want the donut to disappear so it looks like it has been collected by our alien. To do that, place a *hide* looks block inside the condition. To get a new donut to collect, add a *wait (__) seconds* control block and then a *go to (random position)* motion block. (Letting the computer choose a random position will make it more fun because we won't know where the next donut will appear!) Finally, remember that we hid that donut, so even though it's in a new spot, we won't *see* it unless we also add a *show* looks block.

## STEP 3

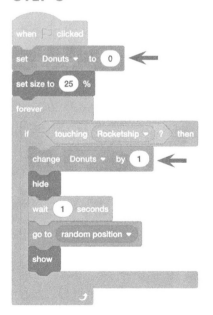

Let's use a variable to help the alien keep track of how many she has. Create a new variable called *Donuts*. Place a *set (Donuts) to (0)* variable block right under your existing *when flag clicked* event block so the number of donuts collected resets to zero every time the game is restarted.

Then add a *change (Donuts) by (1)* variable block right inside your existing *If (touching (Rocketship)?) then* control block so the value of your donut variable increases each time a donut is collected.

## STEP 4: CODE COMPLETE!

As we are counting donuts, we need to know when we've collected as many as we can. To do that, we need to use a condition to write the rule: *If the alien has collected 5 donuts, say "We're all full!"*

 **Click on your rocket ship thumbnail to get to its script editor.** Drag in a new *when flag clicked* event block to start a new script. Add a *forever* control block and place an *If (__) then* control block inside it. Then drag a *(__) = (__)* operator block into the hexagon shape. Place your *Donuts* variable into the first oval and type the number 5 into the second oval. Add a *say (__) for (__) seconds* looks block inside your condition, and type "We're all full!" in the text box.

**DONUT CODE**

**ROCKET CODE**

**7**

## YOUR TURN!

Now that you've coded this activity, try challenging yourself to make the following changes:

☐ Add a fun sound effect for each time a donut is collected.

☐ Add some motion to the donut sprites to make them harder to collect.

☐ Add a timer to the game.

# Conditions Off-Screen

You face a condition with every choice you make. All of those possible paths are *If . . . then statements*, where you weigh the consequences of every action. For example, if you study for your test, you will get a good grade. If you eat too many donuts, your stomach will hurt.

Every time you press numbers on a keypad or type in a password, your device is following a condition, too. For example, "If the password is correct, let them in!"

# Exploring More!

**7**

Conditions are the key to making your programs fun for your user. Everyone likes being able to make choices that lead to different outcomes! Conditions can be used to create anything you can imagine. We can use conditions to build a choose-your-own-adventure story, where the user gets to decide what choices the characters will make or a salon where you get to put different hairstyles on the sprites. You could even use conditions to make a review quiz to help you study for a test at school!

# Hacker Hints

**1** If you right-click on a script in your program, you'll see an option to "Add Comment." This lets you make notes as you work on your code, which can help you stay organized. You can label scripts, explaining what they are supposed to do. You can also use comments to mark sections that you want to work on later.

**2** There's often more than one way to do something in coding. For example, in Activity 2, you used conditions to make the arrow keys control the alien's movements. However, you could also use a variable, like how we made Pufferfish speed up and stop in our last chapter. Another code block that would work is a *when (__) pressed* event block. Check out the scripts below and consider which strategy you like best.

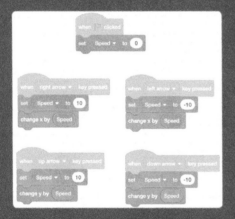

There's not always just "one right way" to make your scripts work. As you gain more experience with coding, you'll learn that you like some ways better because they are easier or more efficient or because they give you more options for other things you may want to add to your program.

7

# Coder's Checklist

You learned lots of helpful things in this chapter, including how to:

- ☐ Use a condition to verify an answer is correct

- ☐ Use a condition to control a sprite's movements and behavior

- ☐ Use commands to sense when a key is being pressed

- ☐ Use commands to sense when sprites make contact with one another

- ☐ Make the movements of a sprite random

Remember, if any of these lessons feel a little unclear, you can always flip back and reread this chapter.

7

# 8

# Data Types and Structures

If data is information, **data types** are the different *kinds* of information you can have in your program. In Scratch, data types are numbers, strings, and Booleans.

Numbers are whole numbers, and we've used these to tell our computer which x- and y-coordinates our sprites needed to move to.

Strings are groups of characters. We've used strings every time we told the computer what text we want to appear in a sprite's word bubble.

Booleans are variables that only have two possible values: true or false. We used these in our last chapter to create all of our conditions.

**Data structures** are how we *organize* our different data types. Think of it as the *layout* for the information. Information itself doesn't change if we move it from one type of data structure to another. But the way we view and access the information *does* change.

Pretend you are studying for a test at school. You could write each fact on a separate index card. You could place all the information in one big outline. You could list the terms in a table. The facts that you are studying don't change, but the different ways you could organize those facts are different data structures.

Scratch has a really cool data structure that lets you store lots of variables at once. It is called a **list**, and that's exactly what it looks like.

Remember how we talked about variables being like boxes that can store information? Well, each numbered item on your list is a separate box for a variable. In our list, number 1 could be *shirts*. And number 2 could be *pants*. And number 3 could be *shoes*. The *types* of shirt, pants, and shoes are all values that can change based on what your user selects. Then your computer can find what type of clothing it can choose from in its list whenever it needs it.

# Data Types and Structures in Scratch

Now that we've learned about lists, let's explore some ways that lists can be useful in Scratch!

# Activity 1—Food Truck Fun

LEVEL UP!

Have you ever ordered food and the person taking your order wrote down everything you said? They wanted to make sure that they had your order right—otherwise they could mishear you and give you boiled squids instead of boiled noodles! Let's use a list to help our food truck get your order right so that you get a delicious meal.

## STEP 1

First, bring in Food Truck sprite.

## STEP 2

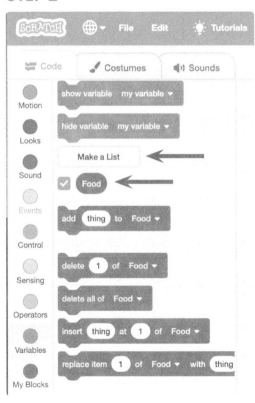

Go to the Variables section of your code menu. Below all the variable code blocks is the option *"Make a List."* Click on this option and name your list "Food." After you've created your list, you will see an oval *Food* code block, and a new section of list code will appear below it.

8

## STEP 3

To start the script, drag out a *when flag clicked* event block. To take the order, first we'll add an *ask (___) and wait* sensing block. Type in, "What would you like to drink?"

Next, drag in an **add (___) to Food** list block. In the first text box, it says "thing." Drag an *answer* sensing block into it. This tells our program to add whatever text the user types to your Food list right here.

---

## STEP 4

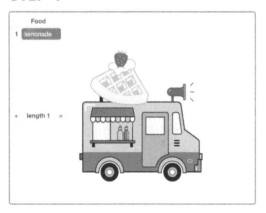

Did you notice that when you created your list, a box suddenly appeared on your stage? This box is showing you what's in your list so far. Right now, it will say that it's empty. Think of it like a notepad—this is where the food truck will take down your order!

Run your program and check that whatever drink you type as an answer shows up as number 1 in the box on your stage.

## STEP 5

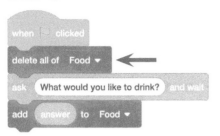

To clear out the list every time the program restarts, you need to place a *delete all of (Food)* list block (you can find this under the *Variables* list) right under your *when flag clicked* event block. That means the first answer typed in will go in the number-1 slot every time you run the program.

## STEP 6

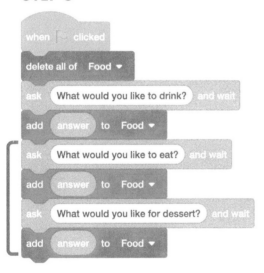

To collect more information for your list, add another *ask (__) and wait* sensing block to ask what they would like to eat and an *add (__) to Food* list block to add the user's new response to the list.

Then add a final *ask (__) and wait* sensing block to ask what they would like for dessert and an *add (__) to Food* list block to add the user's new response to the list. Order up!

8

## STEP 7: CODE COMPLETE!

Now run your program. Notice that your computer will add all your answers to the list. Now you can see everything that you ordered!

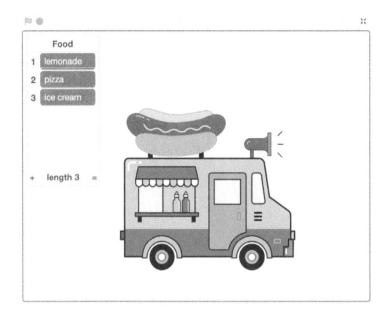

## YOUR TURN!

Now that you've coded this activity, try challenging yourself to make the following changes:

☐ Add more questions for the food truck to ask.

☐ Add a sprite who walks up to the food truck to give their order.

☐ Make the new sprite ask some questions, and create a new list for their responses. What could you make them say?

# Activity 2—Ask Wizard Toad

Let me introduce you to the wizard toad. This magical amphibian is well known for giving advice to anyone who comes to him with questions, but he needs a *list* to share his wisdom. In this activity, we'll be creating a list on the front end for our sprite to use. Ready to test his magic? Let's go!

----

## STEP 1

Choose Wizard Toad from your sprite library.

----

## STEP 2

Create a list, and name it "Advice." (Remember, the option to make a new list is found in the *Variable* section of your code menu.) The new list will appear on your stage. To add new possible responses to your list, click the plus sign on the bottom left side of the box, and an orange text box will pop up. Let's type "Great idea!" Keep clicking the plus sign to add more. You can copy the responses pictured here or get creative and come up with your own ideas—you'll need five possible options. This list will store all of the possible responses he can give to our questions!

8

## STEP 3

Now drag in a *when flag clicked* event block and an *ask ( __ ) and wait* sensing block to have the wizard toad ask, "What is your question?" Then add a *say ( __ ) for ( __ ) seconds* looks block and place an *item ( __ ) of (Advice)* list block inside its text box.

---

## STEP 4

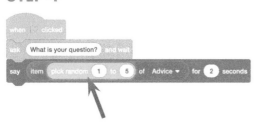

You don't want Wizard Toad to give the same advice every time. *Boring!* Instead, you want him to give a random response from his list of possibilities. To make his response random, place a *pick random ( __ ) to ( __ )* operator block in the item number space of your *item ( __ ) of (Advice)* list block. The default numbers are between 1 and 10. Since you only have five possible responses, change the numbers to between 1 and 5.

8

## STEP 5: CODE COMPLETE!

The last thing to do is place a *hide list Advice* list block right under your *when flag clicked* event block so the possible responses stay hidden. We want them to be a surprise!

Now whenever you need some advice, just ask the good old wizard toad!

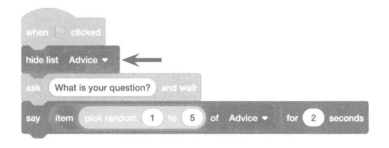

---

## YOUR TURN!

Now that you've coded this activity, try challenging yourself to make the following changes:

☐ Add a costume change for Wizard Toad when he is answering your question.

☐ Add a magic ball sprite for Wizard Toad to look into to find the answers.

☐ Make the ball change colors to look more magical.

8

# Activity 3—Lucky Guess!

Nano is a funny little creature who loves guessing games. She has three favorite colors. Can you guess one of them? This time we have to place code that tells the computer to *check* Nano's list and then compare it with whatever answer the user gives.

---

## STEP 1

Bring in Nano sprite. Check out all of her costumes and see which you like the best. We've used Nano-c!

---

## STEP 2

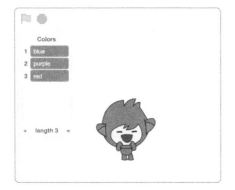

Make a new list, and name it *"Colors."* Add Nano's three favorite colors. For now, let's choose blue, purple, and red—but you can pick anything you want.

Next, place a *when flag clicked* event block and a **hide list Colors** list block. (If you need to see your list again later, you can just click on the **show list Colors** block from your code menu.) Then use an *ask (__) and wait* sensing block to have Nano say, "Try guessing one of my favorite colors."

To code this activity, we need to make a rule. The rule is that if the user guesses a word that is on our list, Nano will let them know they guessed one of her favorites. If the user guesses wrong, Nano will tell them they are wrong. Can you remember which kind of coding tool we need to make a rule?

That's right! A *condition*.

---

## STEP 3

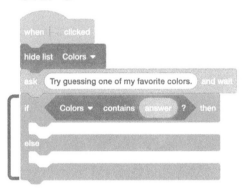

In this case, we need an *If (___) then (___) else (___)* control block. Add one to your script and place the hexagon-shaped *Colors contains (___) ?* list block inside it. The computer needs to figure out if what the user types matches anything on your *Colors* list, so drag an *answer* sensing block into the text box of the list block you just added.

You have just written the first part of your rule, which is *If the Color list contains the answer given by the user then . . .* Now what should Nano do?

8

## STEP 4: CODE COMPLETE!

Now use a *say (__) for (__) seconds* looks blocks to make Nano let you know if you answered correctly. You can use the response pictured here or make up your own! Use an *answer* sensing block to make Nano restate whatever you typed for an answer. Use a *join (__) (__)* operator block to connect the *answer* sensing block with the text that you type in for Nano to speak.

Now let's code Nano's response for guessing *incorrectly*. You can repeat the same code blocks we just used, but this time change the statement to "Nope, I don't like *(answer)*."

When Nano speaks, do you notice that some words are smushed together? You will need to add a space at the end of the text box so that the last word you typed won't be smushed together with the text stored in the *answer* sensing block.

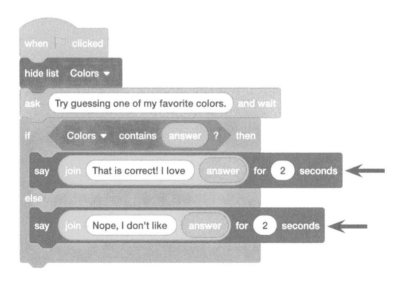

Great work! See if you can stump your friends with Nano's guessing game!

## YOUR TURN!

Now that you've coded this activity, try challenging yourself to make the following changes:

☐ Nano has so many cute costumes. Have her change costumes depending on whether the user guesses correctly.

☐ If the user guesses one of the correct answers, make the backdrop change to match that color.

☐ Make a new list with something different for the user to guess.

# Data Types and Structures Off-Screen

Have you ever purchased a snack from a vending machine? You can see that the food is hanging on long metal rods, with the same types all hanging in a row together. Other rods contain other choices, but each rod only contains *one* type of snack. Each rod also has a number on it or sometimes a letter and number combo like C5. Think of the vending machine as your data structure. The label on each rod is like the name of a variable. And the snack hanging on the rod is the value of that variable. If you want the peanut butter crackers, you let the machine know your choice by punching in its variable name. Then there's a little whirl, and the machine drops the snack! Pretty clever, huh?

8

# Exploring More!

Remember that the items in your list are all variables. That means their values can change whenever you need them to. Think about other things you could store and why you might need to get that information later in your scripts. For example, what if your sprite could collect different items and they were recorded in a list? Then you could track his "inventory," so when he goes to the market, he knows what items he has available to sell for coins.

# Hacker Hints

**1** As you've learned, each *say (__) for (__) seconds* looks block will create a word bubble for your sprite. If you put a lot of text in that one code block, you will have one *giant* word bubble. It might take up most of the stage! And seeing a huge block of text can feel really overwhelming for your user to read. To fix this, add more *say (__) for (__) seconds* looks blocks and split the text between them. Then the sprite will speak in several word bubbles. *Much better!*

**2** Need to make some changes to your list? Maybe you don't like the fortune you wrote for Wizard Toad in the number 3 slot:

☐ Use a *delete (__) of (__)* list block to delete a specific slot on your list.

☐ Use an *insert (__) at (__) of (__)* list block to add a new variable in a certain spot on your list. Be aware, if you insert something in slot number 2, the original slot number 2 will shift down to become number 3, and the rest of the list will also shift down too.

☐ If you want to *change* the value of number 2 without moving any other values into different slots, then you can use the *replace item (__) of (__) with (__)* list block.

8

# Coder's Checklist

You learned lots of cool things in this chapter, including how to:

☐ Add values to and remove values from a list

☐ Report values from a list

☐ Randomize responses from a list, like you did with Wizard Toad

☐ Check to see if data matches values from a list, like when you guessed Nano's favorite color

☐ Show and hide a list

Remember, if any of these feel unclear, you can always flip back and reread this chapter.

8

# 9

# Event Handling

**Event handling** is how you create "triggers" so things start happening in your programs. Once you set off an event, the computer knows to follow the script that's attached to that event. Events also allow your scripts to communicate with each other so the computer can switch from one script to another in a certain order.

You've already used the *when flag clicked* event block to start your programs. When the user clicks the green flag, it sets off the *when flag clicked* event block, and then the computer knows to follow all of the directions attached to that event.

However, we can use other kinds of triggers in our program. For example, Scratch has a *when this sprite clicked* event block. This means that you can write a script that the computer only follows after the user clicks on a sprite. Pretty cool, huh?

There's also a type of event called a **broadcast**. These are signals that can be sent out from one script and then be received by others. We use the *broadcast (___)* event block to send a signal, and we use the *when I receive (___)* event block to start a new script. It's kind of like using a walkie-talkie. When you speak into a walkie-talkie, you are sending out a signal, and anyone else with a walkie-talkie can *receive* it.

# Event Handling in Scratch

Using events like broadcasting opens up so much more that you can do with your programs. Let's try it out!

# Activity 1—The Incredible Size-Changing Starfish

Meet the Incredible Starfish. He can grow and shrink, all with the click of a button. We just need to use our events to trigger those buttons so Starfish can receive his broadcasted messages and follow your commands!

------------------------------------------------------------

**STEP 1**

Bring in the Starfish sprite and two Ball sprites. To make the second ball green, simply click on its green costume option in the Costumes tab.

## STEP 2

**Click on the thumbnail of the green ball below the stage to open its script editor.** Start your script with a *when this sprite clicked* event block. Then add a *broadcast ( )* event block. Click on the drop-down menu in the code block and choose "New message." Type in "Shrink."

Try clicking on your green button. Starfish isn't doing any shrinking, is he? Well, we have *sent* a broadcast. But we have not told Starfish to *receive* it yet.

---

## STEP 3

**Click on Starfish's thumbnail to open up his script editor.** Add a *when I receive ( )* event block and choose "Shrink" from the drop-down menu.

Now Starfish has received the broadcast, but we also have to tell him what he is supposed to do! You want him to get smaller, so you need to add a *change size by ( )* looks block. Type in -10 for the number, so every time he receives the broadcast, he will shrink by 10% of his size. Try it out! Can you make Starfish shrink? Nice job!

## STEP 4: CODE COMPLETE!

To make Starfish grow, go ahead and program the yellow ball to send a "Grow" broadcast. When Starfish receives the broadcast, he needs to increase his size by 10%. We'll write the same code that we did in Step 3, but what number do you think you'll place in the change size by spot? 10, right? If -10 made the green ball shrink by 10%, 10 will make Starfish grow by 10%.

Now the Starfish can grow and shrink at the click of a mouse! Great work—you just used two new event types! You made your sprites follow a script when they were clicked on, and you sent out broadcasts to trigger new scripts to run!

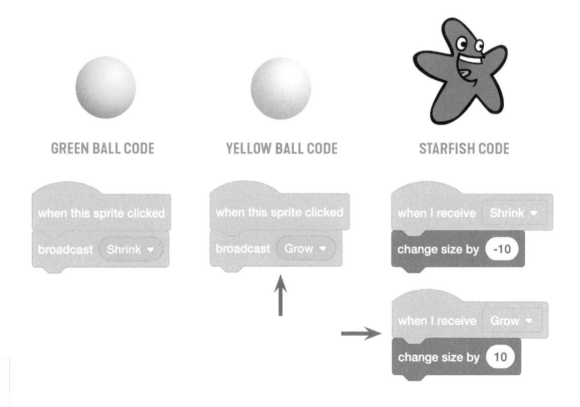

GREEN BALL CODE          YELLOW BALL CODE          STARFISH CODE

# YOUR TURN!

Now that you've coded this activity, try challenging yourself to make the following changes:

☐ Make Starfish reset to 100% of his size when the flag is clicked.

☐ Add different sound effects for when Starfish is growing or shrinking.

☐ Use variables to make Starfish warn the user when he is getting too small or too big.

# Activity 2—Knock, Knock!

LEVEL UP!

Did you know dinosaurs love a good knock-knock joke? Well, these dinosaurs definitely do! And a knock-knock joke is the perfect way to practice sending multiple broadcasts.

---

## STEP 1

Bring in the green Dinosaur1 sprite and the red Dinosaur2 sprite.

---

## STEP 2

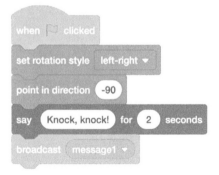

**Go to the red dinosaur's script editor.**
Start his script with a *when flag clicked* event block. Then add a *set rotation style (left-right)* motion block and a *point in direction (-90)* motion block to make him face the other dinosaur.

Add a *say (___) for (___) seconds* looks block and type "Knock, knock!" Then add a *broadcast (___)* event block. The default will be "message1." Let's leave that for now. It actually doesn't matter what we call this message—it won't be what the dinosaur is saying. Instead, it's just a trigger to set off the next action.

Now that the red dinosaur has started the joke, we need the green dinosaur to respond. Luckily, our red dinosaur sent out a broadcast. That means our green dinosaur can *receive* it, and that will trigger his response.

---

## STEP 3

**Go to the green dinosaur's script editor.**
Start with a *when I receive (message1)* event block and add a *say (__) for (__) seconds* looks block to have him ask, "Who's there?"

Then the green dinosaur needs to send out a *new* broadcast. Add a *broadcast (__)* event block. For our last broadcast, we used the preset message. This time, we need a brand-new signal, so we must create a new message. When naming your broadcasts, the key is to stay well organized. The names will help you with your own planning. For this broadcast, click on *New message* and then name it "message2." We'll keep adding a number to each new broadcast we create to keep the broadcasts in order.

## STEP 4

Now it's time for the joke! You can program in any knock-knock joke you want or follow along here.

**Go to the red dinosaur's script editor.**
He can be triggered to respond with a *when I receive (___)* event block. Click on the arrow and choose "message2." Then add a *say (___) for (___) seconds* looks block to have him say, "Tank!" Finally, add a *broadcast (___)* event block to send a trigger to our other dinosaur. Name this new broadcast "message3."

## STEP 5

**Go to the green dinosaur's script editor.** Can you program his response? He needs to receive the message3 broadcast "Tank who?" and send a message4 broadcast back to the red dinosaur.

## STEP 6: CODE COMPLETE!

Ready for the punch line? **Go to the red dinosaur's script editor.** Make him receive the message4 broadcast and say "You're welcome!"

Get it? Such a polite dinosaur!

**RED DINOSAUR CODE**

**GREEN DINOSAUR CODE**

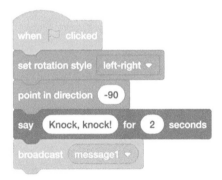

## YOUR TURN!

Now that you've coded this activity, try challenging yourself to make the following changes:

☐ Add a laugh soundtrack that plays after the punch line.

☐ Use a broadcast to trigger a third sprite who enters after the joke.

☐ Have the new sprite tell their own joke.

# Activity 3—Flying Ball Thief

So far, so good with event handling! Now let's try something more challenging. Let's build a scene where two boys are kicking a ball back and forth, and then a giant bird swoops down from the sky and carries their ball off! Can we use some events to make that happen? Let's try it out!

## STEP 1

Bring in Dee, Devin, Parrot, and Soccer Ball. Then add the Woods and Bench backdrop. Position the boys and the ball like you see here. Feel free to change their costumes if you want!

For this program, it is very important to use the *broadcast ( ) and wait* event block. Since we will be sending multiple broadcasts in the *same* script, we want the computer to *wait* until everyone receives and acts on a broadcast *before* we send out the *next* broadcast in the list. If you use regular broadcasts without a wait, they all get sent so quickly that the sprites will be reacting almost at the same time, and that will really mess up our timing!

## STEP 2

**Start with Dee's script editor.** Begin with a *when flag clicked* event block. Then use *set rotation style (left-right)* and *point in direction (-90)* motion blocks to turn him to face Devin.

Next, we'll add a list of broadcasts to outline everything that will happen in our scene. Dee can send out *all* of the broadcasts for us, and then other sprites can receive them to act out the scene.

We need to make three broadcasts for our scene:

The first is "kick ball" to get the ball rolling.

The next is "bird fly in" so our bird can appear on the stage and swoop down.

The last is "bird take ball" so that our bird can grab the ball and carry it away off the stage!

Remember to use the *broadcast (___) and wait* event block.

Now that we have an outline for our scene, the next step is to have our sprites receive these broadcasts and take action!

## STEP 3

**Go to the soccer ball's script editor.**
Begin with a *when flag clicked* event block, a *show* looks block, and a *set size to ( )* % looks block. Change the size of the soccer ball to 75% so it will look more realistic compared to the size of the boys.

## STEP 4

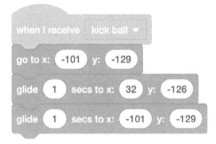

Now start a second script for your soccer ball with a *when I receive ( )* event block and choose "kick ball" from the list. Your ball is already positioned at Devin's feet, so go ahead and drag in a *go to x: ( ) y: ( )* motion block to set its starting position.

Then click the ball and drag it to Dee's feet. Add a *glide ( ) secs to x: ( ) y: ( )* motion block.

Next, click the ball and drag it back to Devin's feet. Add another *glide ( ) secs to x: ( ) y: ( )* motion block.

Run your program, and the ball should now move from Devin to Dee and then back to Devin.

## STEP 5

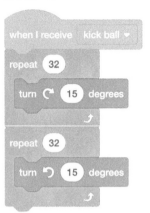

Now let's make the ball spin! We want the ball to spin *while* it's gliding, so you need to add a new *when I receive (__)* event block and choose "kick ball" from the list. This creates two different scripts with the *same* trigger. To make the ball spin, use *repeat* control blocks and *turn (__)* motion blocks. You will want the ball to turn to the right when it is moving toward Dee and to the left when it's moving back toward Devin. Play around with the number of repeats until the ball is spinning the right amount of times. (Tip: if your ball isn't spinning, change your rotation style to "all around.")

## STEP 6

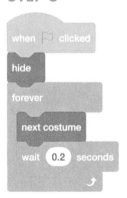

**Go to the bird's script editor.** The first thing we need is for the bird to be hiding at the beginning of our program. We can also go ahead and program him to flap his wings. Since he starts out hidden, it won't matter if his wings start flapping right away.

Add a *when flag clicked* event block and a **hide** looks block. Then place a *forever* control block around a **next costume** looks block and a *wait (__)* control block. You want a small wait, like 0.2 seconds.

# STEP 7

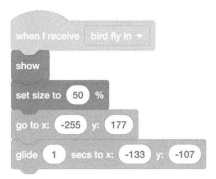

To code the bird's movements, start a new script with a *when I receive (__)* event block. Choose "bird fly in" from your list. You first need to add a *show* looks block so the bird will be visible after he receives the broadcast. Use your mouse to drag your bird up to the top-left corner so he is just peeking into the stage. Add a *go to x: (__) y: (__)* motion block. Then drag your bird down near Devin's feet, right where the ball stops rolling. Add a *glide (__) secs to x: (__) y: (__)* motion block.

Now the bird should swoop in and stop right above the ball.

---

# STEP 8

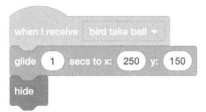

For the bird to take the ball, start a new script with a *when I receive (__)* event block. This time, choose "bird take ball" from your list. Use your mouse to drag the bird up to the top-right corner and then drag in a *glide (__) secs to x: (__) y: (__)* motion block. Finish with a *hide* looks block so the bird will seem to disappear off into the distance with his stolen soccer ball.

To make it look like the ball was snatched, you need the ball to receive the *same* broadcast and then have it move up to the right with the bird and disappear.

---

## STEP 9: CODE COMPLETE!

**DEE CODE**

**Go back to your ball's script editor.** Start a new script with a *when I receive (__)* event block and choose "bird take ball" from your list. Move your ball up to the same spot where you made your bird disappear and add a *glide (__) secs to x: (__) y: (__)* motion block. Finally, finish with a *hide* looks block.

Play your program several times and adjust your x- and y-coordinates until the ball looks like it's being carried away by the bird. Here, the ball's final x-coordinate had to be 50 *more* than the bird's x-coordinate, and the ball's y-coordinate had to be 40 *less* than the bird's y-coordinate.

Now you have a sneaky ball thief. What a tricky bird!

## BIRD CODE

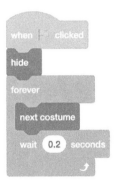

when 🏳 clicked
hide
forever
    next costume
    wait 0.2 seconds

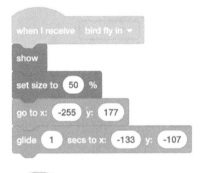

when I receive bird fly in ▾
show
set size to 50 %
go to x: -255 y: 177
glide 1 secs to x: -133 y: -107

when I receive bird take ball ▾
glide 1 secs to x: 300 y: 110
hide

## BALL CODE

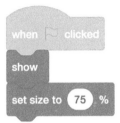

when 🏳 clicked
show
set size to 75 %

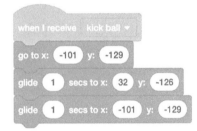

when I receive kick ball ▾
go to x: -101 y: -129
glide 1 secs to x: 32 y: -126
glide 1 secs to x: -101 y: -129

when I receive kick ball ▾
repeat 32
    turn ↻ 15 degrees
repeat 32
    turn ↺ 15 degrees

when I receive bird take ball ▾
glide 1 secs to x: 250 y: 150
hide

Now that you've coded this activity, try challenging yourself to make the following changes:

☐ Program the boys to react to the ball theft.

☐ Program the bird to fly back over with the ball, taunting the boys.

☐ Program the bird to come back one more time and drop the ball for the boys.

# Event Handling Off-Screen

You've definitely seen event handling in your real life—have you ever passed a note to a friend? You folded it up and sent your note out into the world. Your friend got the note, and then they took action. Maybe they just wrote a response and passed it back to you. Or maybe your note said, "Hey, you have a milk mustache!" and so they grabbed a napkin and wiped their face. That was just like sending a broadcast. A message was sent, and whoever received the message was triggered to take action!

# Exploring More!

Broadcasts can be sent at any time during a program, and they can be received by multiple sprites. In fact, a sprite can even receive his own broadcasts that he sent out. Now that you have this tool, think about how you could use broadcasts to trigger cool things to happen in your games! Remember your alien who was collecting donuts? What if every time she collected a donut, a broadcast also got sent out? What new sprites might receive the broadcast? What could you make happen?

# Hacker Hints

It's important to stay organized when you are working with broadcasts. Make sure that the name of the broadcast being sent matches the name of the broadcast being *received*. Pay attention to when you want to use a *broadcast (__)* command versus a *broadcast (__) and wait* command. It all depends on how you want the timing of your program to work!

# Coder's Checklist

You learned lots of important things in this chapter, including:

☐ How to use the *when this sprite clicked* event

☐ How to send *broadcast* events to multiple sprites

☐ How to receive *broadcast* events

☐ When to use *broadcast (__) and wait* events

Remember, if any of these feel a little unclear, you can always flip back and reread this chapter.

# 10

# Game On: Putting It All Together

Now that you have a full toolbox, let's have some fun putting together everything you've learned in a game!

# Game On!

# Fire-Breathing Wand Quest!

A wizard has lost his wand! Luckily, his wizard friend found it, but she needs your help to return it—because guess who found the wand *first*? A dragon—and he doesn't want to give it back!

   Let's create a game where the wizard who found the wand asks for help fighting the dragon. First, she will ask you your name and where you are from. Then she'll explain how you can help her get around with your mouse and use the space bar to throw lightning bolts at the dragon. After five successful hits, the dragon will give up. Then our wizard can grab the wand and take it back to her friend, who will be very grateful!

-------------------------------------------------------------------------------

## STEP 1

Bring in the Mountain backdrop, Wizard Girl sprite, Wand sprite, Lightning sprite, and Dragon sprite. Position them like you see here.

## STEP 2

**Start with Wizard Girl's script editor.**
We want her to ask some questions, and we can store your answers in a *list*, so begin by making a list called "*User Info*." Then drag out a *when flag clicked* event block to start the script. Add a *delete all of (User Info)* list block so our data clears out whenever we start a new game. Now let's position Wizard Girl by adding a *go to x: (__) y (__)* motion block. Add a *switch backdrop to (Mountain)* looks block to set the background. Then add a *show* looks block to make Wizard Girl visible.

Now add an *ask (__) and wait* sensing block, so we can write Wizard Girl's questions. Type "Hello! Please tell me your name!" in the text box. Next, add an *add (__) to (User Info)* list block. To store the response to the question in your list, drag an *answer* sensing block into the list block so it now says *add (answer) to (User Info)*. Create the next question with a second *ask (__) and wait* sensing block, and type "And what state do you come from?" in the text box. Then create a second *add (answer) to (User Info)* list block to store the second answer in your list. Once you know your list is working properly, remove the check mark next to "User Info" in your code menu so it will no longer show up on your stage.

**10**

## STEP 3

```
when [ ] clicked
delete all of   User Info ▼
go to x:  -145  y:  1
switch backdrop to   Mountain ▼
show
ask   Hello! Please tell me your name!   and wait
add   answer   to   User Info ▼
ask   And what state do you come from?   and wait
add   answer   to   User Info ▼
say   I have found the missing wand, but I need your help!   for  2  seconds
say   Use your mouse to move me up and down.   for  2  seconds
say   Press space bar to shoot lightning!   for  2  seconds
broadcast   Start Game ▼   and wait
```

Now, we'll program Wizard Girl's responses to your answers and let her explain the rules of our game. Add three *say (__) for (__) seconds* looks blocks. In the first block, type "I have found the missing wand, but I need your help!" In the second block, type "Use your mouse to move me up and down." In the third block, type "Press space bar to shoot lightning!" Then finish by adding a *broadcast (__) and wait* event block. Name it "Start Game."

## STEP 4

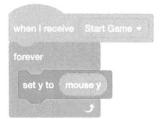

```
when I receive   Start Game ▼
forever
  set y to   mouse y
```

When the game begins, we want Wizard Girl to move up and down with your mouse, but not forward. Stay in Wizard Girl's script editor, drag in a *when I receive (__)* event block, and choose Start Game from the drop-down menu. Add a *forever* control block. Place a *set y to (__)* motion block inside the loop. Then place a *mouse y* sensing command inside the motion block.

**10**

This loop will cause Wizard Girl's y-coordinate to always match whatever the y-coordinate of your mouse is. Her x-coordinate will stay the same, which means she can't move forward—that's good because we don't want her to run into the dragon!

## STEP 5

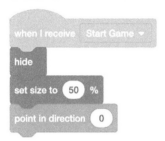

**Now let's move on to the lightning sprite's script editor!** We want the lightning to shoot out from Wizard Girl and fly *toward* the dragon. First, use a *when I receive (Start Game)* event block. Add a *hide* looks block so we don't see the lightning until we are ready to shoot it. Add a *set size to (50) %* looks block to shrink the lightning. Then add a *point in direction (0)* motion block. This will make it fly out from Wizard Girl, parallel to the ground.

## STEP 6

To make the lightning actually *move*, start a new script with a *when (space) key pressed* event block. Add a *show* looks block so the lightning only appears when we're ready for her to throw it. Since Wizard Girl is following your mouse, the lightning needs a *set y to (__)* motion block, with a *mouse y* sensing command inside the motion block so that the lightning will *also* start from wherever your mouse is. That way, it will always appear to be shooting from Wizard Girl.

10

Then add a *repeat (___)* control block and place a *change x by (10)* motion block inside the block so the lightning will fly straight out toward the dragon. To figure out the number of repeats in the loop, start with 30 and then experiment to see how many repeats you need to get the lightning to travel across your screen. Then add a *hide* looks block. Finally, add a *go to (___)* motion block and choose "Wizard Girl" from the drop-down menu so the lightning will return to her, ready to go again!

---

## STEP 7

Now let's program the dragon! **Go to the dragon's script editor.** Start with a *when I receive (Start Game)* event block. Then add a *show* looks block so the dragon appears when he gets that broadcast. Next, add a *switch costume to (dragon-b)* looks block. Right now he's pretty big, which means he'll be *too* easy to hit. Use a *set size to (50) %* looks block to shrink him. We also need him to face Wizard Girl, so add a *set rotation style (left-right)* and a *point in direction (-90)* motion block. Then set his position with a *go to x: (___) y: (___)* motion block.

We'll need to create a variable to track the number of times the lightning hits the dragon. Let's name it "*Hits*." Add a *show variable (Hits)* variable block to your script and a *set (Hits) to (0)* variable block so we start over each time we run the program.

# STEP 8

Let's make this dragon move! Start a new script for him with a *when I receive (Start Game)* event block. He will receive the same broadcast as he did in Step 6, so these new directions will happen at the same time. To make the dragon move and dodge our lightning, add a *forever* control block and a *glide (__) secs to x: (__) y: (__)* motion block. We want the dragon's movements to be random, but we don't want him going all over—he needs to stay close to guard the wand! Use a *pick random (__) to (__)* operator block for *each* of your coordinates. For your x-coordinate, choose from 54 to 195, and for your y-coordinate, choose from 88 to -76. This will keep him in just one area of the screen but still let him move randomly. To speed up his movements, change his glide time to 0.25 seconds.

We need a condition to make the rule that every time the lightning touches the dragon, our Hits variable will increase, and our dragon will breathe fire! Add an *if (__) then* event block and place a *touching (__) ?* sensing block inside the hexagon shape. Choose "lightning" from the drop-down menu in the sensing block. Then add a *change (Hits) by 1* variable block inside the event block. Next, we need a *switch costume to (dragon-c)* looks block to make him breathe fire. Add a *wait (1) seconds* control block and then a *switch costume to (dragon-b)* looks block so he resets to his original costume.

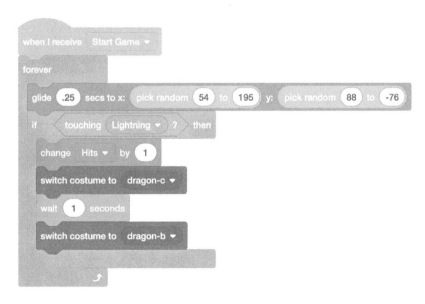

10

## STEP 9

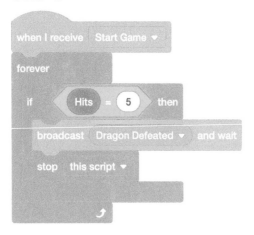

Now let's make a rule that once the dragon is hit five times, he will give up and fly away. Start a new script for him with a *when I receive (Start Game)* event block. Add a *forever* control block. Add an *if (__) then* control block and place a *(__) = (__)* operator block inside its hexagon shape. Place a *Hits* variable block into the first circle of the operator block. Type "5" into the second circle. Then place a *broadcast (__) and wait* event block inside the condition. Name the broadcast: "Dragon Defeated." Finally, add something new: a *stop (__)* control block. Choose "this script" from the drop-down menu.

Okay, what was that new kind of code block we just used, and why did we need it?

Well, we sent a broadcast, but it was *inside* a *forever* control block. That means that the broadcast will keep being sent over and over again, forever! But we only want it to get sent *one* time. So we needed a *stop (__)* control block. The preset value was "all," which means it would end *all* the scripts in your program. We didn't want that. So, instead, we chose "this script." This way, after the broadcast is sent, all the commands in just that script will stop. This is a way to basically "kill" scripts that you don't need for the rest of your program, and it's very helpful when working with forever loops. Sometimes you want "forever" to really just mean "forever for a little while"!

10

## STEP 10

Next, we'll program what happens *after* we defeat our tricky dragon! Start a new script in your dragon script editor with a *when I receive (Dragon Defeated)* event block and add a *hide variable (Hits)* variable block. Then use a *say (\_\_) for (2) seconds* looks blocks to make him say, "Drat! You can have it!" Drag your dragon to the top of your screen and then add a *glide (\_\_) secs to x: (\_\_) y: (\_\_)* motion block and a *hide* looks block so he will fly away, off-screen. Last, add a *broadcast (\_\_) and wait* event block. Name it "Get Wand."

---

## STEP 11

**Go back to Wizard Girl's script editor.** Let's program her to grab that wand! Start a new script with a *when I receive (Get Wand)* event block. We don't want her to follow our mouse up and down anymore, so use the *stop (\_\_)* control block we learned about in Step 8. This time, choose "other scripts in sprite" from the drop-down menu. This means we will "kill" all of her earlier scripts, causing anything we placed in a forever loop to stop working.

Drag her to the bottom-right side of the stage, right on top of the wand. Add a *glide (\_\_) secs to x: (\_\_) y: (\_\_)* motion block so that she will move from her position to the wand. Add a *hide* looks block so she leaves the scene. Finally, add a *broadcast (\_\_) and wait* event block. Name this "Return the Wand."

**10**

## STEP 12

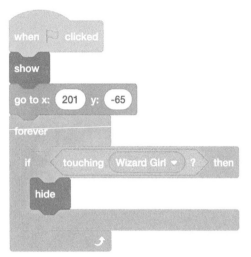

**Now go to the wand's script editor.**
We need to program it to show up at the start of our game and disappear when Wizard Girl grabs it. Start with a *when flag clicked* event block. Then add a *show* looks block. Drag in a *go to x: (__) y: (__)* motion block to set its position. Then add a *forever* control block. Place an *if (__) then* control block inside the loop to set up a condition. We made Wizard Girl glide over and grab the wand in our last step, so we can use that contact to trigger the wand to disappear as if she has collected it. Place a *touching (__) ?* sensing block inside the condition's hexagon shape and choose Wizard Girl in the drop-down. Finally, add a *hide* looks block inside the condition.

10

## STEP 13

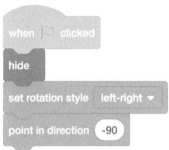

Now Wizard Girl can bring the wand home to her friend! Bring in the Witch House backdrop and the Wizard sprite. We'll call him Wizard Man. Place Wizard Man on the screen like you see here. **Then go to Wizard Man's script editor.** Add a *when flag clicked* event block and a *hide* looks block so he stays hidden for the first part of our game. Let's also use a *set rotation style (left-right)* block and a *point in direction (-90)* motion block to make him face the other direction for when we are ready for him to show again.

## STEP 14

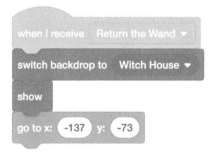

**Return to Wizard Girl's script editor.** Start a new script with a *when I receive (Return the Wand)* events block. Then add a *switch backdrop to (Witch House)* looks block to change our background to the next scene. Add a *show* looks block. Place her on the left-hand side of the stage and drag in a *go to x: (__) y: (__)* motion block to set her position.

10

## STEP 15

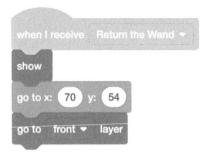

**Now go back to your wand script editor.** We need to program it into our new scene. The wand should receive the same broadcast we used in step 13: *when I receive (Return the Wand)*. Then add a *show* looks block to make the wand visible. Drag the wand into our new wizard friend's hand. (If Wizard Man is hidden, you can click on the Show eyeball icon underneath the stage to make him visible.) Once you have the wand positioned, add a *go to x: (__) y: (__)* motion block to set the position. If your wand is showing up *behind* Wizard Man's hand, try adding a *go to (front) layer* looks block to make it move in front of Wizard Man so it looks like he is holding it.

## STEP 16

Now let's program our wizard to accept the wand from our hero! **Go to Wizard Man's script editor.** Start a new script for him with a *when I receive (Return the Wand)* event block. Add a *show* looks block. Drag in a *go to x: (__) y: (__)* motion block to set his position. Add a *say (__) for (2) seconds* looks block and type in "You found it!" Then add a *broadcast (__) and wait* event block. Name it "I Had Help."

10

## STEP 17

Now let's use that information that we stored in our list at the beginning of our program. **Return to Wizard Girl's script editor.** Start a new script with a *when I receive (I Had Help)* event block. Then add two *say (__) for (2) seconds* looks blocks and place a *join (__) (__)* operator block inside each of them.

Type "I could not have done it without" in the first circle of the first looks block. Then drag an *item (1) of (User Info)* list block into the second text box (this will be your name). In the second looks block, type "They came all the way from" into the first box. Then drag an *item (2) of (User Info)* list block into the second text box (this will be your state). Add a space at the end of each text box so your last word won't be smushed with the text from your list.

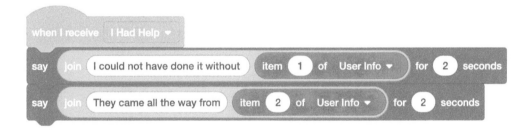

# CODE COMPLETE!

Congratulations, you're a hero! You defeated the dragon, returned the wand, and used *all* the fundamental coding concepts from this book, including loops, variables, conditions, data structures, *and* event handling to make this program work!

## WIZARD GIRL CODE

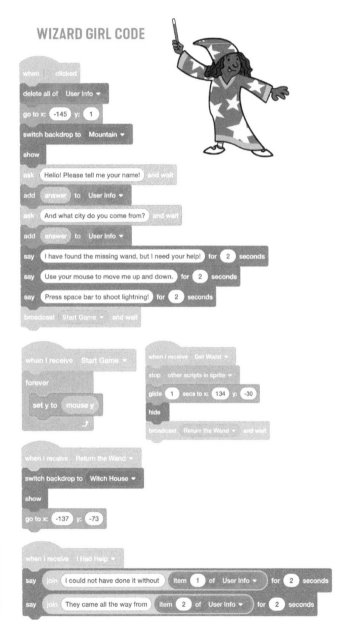

## LIGHTNING CODE

## DRAGON CODE

## WAND CODE

## WIZARD MAN CODE

```
when I receive Start Game
show
switch costume to dragon-b
set size to 50 %
set rotation style left-right
point in direction -90
go to x: 122 y: -34
show variable Hits
set Hits to 0
```

```
when I receive Start Game
forever
  if Hits = 5 then
    broadcast Dragon Defeated and wait
    stop this script
```

```
when I receive Start Game
forever
  glide .25 secs to x: pick random 54 to 195 y: pick random 88 to -76
  if touching Lightning ? then
    change Hits by 1
    switch costume to dragon-c
    wait 1 seconds
    switch costume to dragon-b
```

```
when I receive Dragon Defeated
hide variable Hits
say Drat! You can have it! for 2 seconds
glide 1 secs to x: -147 y: 192
hide
broadcast Get Wand and wait
```

```
when clicked
show
go to x: 201 y: -65
forever
  if touching Wizard Girl ? then
    hide
```

```
when I receive Return the Wand
show
go to x: 70 y: 54
go to front layer
```

```
when clicked
hide
set rotation style left-right
point in direction -90
```

```
when I receive Return the Wand
show
go to x: 109 y: -33
say You found it! for 2 seconds
broadcast I Had Help and wait
```

**10**

# Getting Creative: Design Your Own Game

Now that you understand how to use all of your coding tools, you can design your own games and make anything you can imagine! But while you're designing, make sure your games have all the important ingredients you need to make a great game.

## Game Ingredients

**Objective:** What is the goal of the game? What are you trying to do? For example, in the game we just made, our objective was to return the wand to the wizard.

**Operation:** How do you play the game? In our last game, we were able to move Wizard Girl up and down with our mouse and throw lightning with the space bar. What rules will you create in your own games?

**Obstacles:** What challenge must be overcome? Is there a villain? Or maybe your sprite must jump over hot lava to reach the finish line. In our last game, the dragon was our obstacle.

**Outcome:** What happens so you know you won or lost? In our last game, we knew we had won when the dragon gave up the wand, Wizard Man got his wand back, and Wizard Girl thanked us for our help.

**10**

# Game Challenge: Obstacle Course

So, how would you program a racing game where you press the arrow key to make the sprite run forward and jump over obstacles to make it to the finish line? How can you make the background scroll past so that it feels like a long race, not just a quick run across the stage?

To design this game, remember: think like a programmer. You'll need to tell the computer to move some background elements—like trees and clouds—across the screen whenever the user moves their sprite forward. The elements moving past would create an *illusion* that the sprite is moving forward. You could use lots of different sprites as your background elements or you could use the same ones by telling the computer to hide them when they move off the left side of the screen and then move them back to the right side and show them again. Randomizer code and costume changes can make your background look even more varied!

Consider what could happen if your sprite runs into an obstacle instead of jumping over it. For example, you could use a conditional block, a sensing block, and a broadcast block to send the sprite back to the beginning every time it collides with an obstacle!

With your four important game ingredients in mind, you'll be able to make all kinds of fun games by using your coding toolbox. Isn't it cool to be a *creator*?

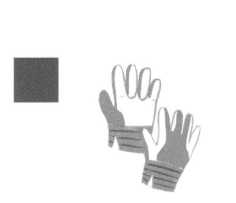

10

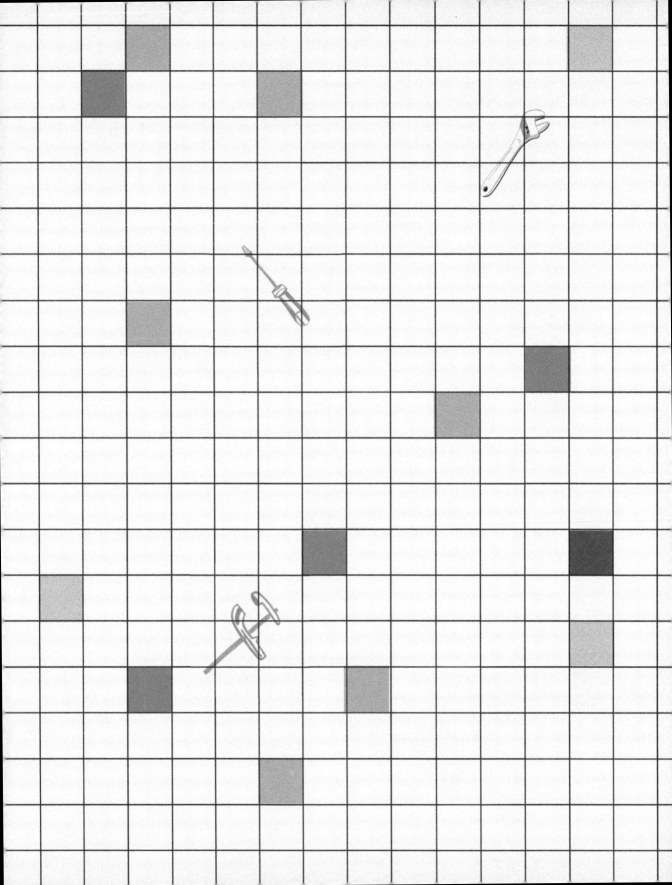

# Code for the Road

Congratulations on finishing this book—you have learned so much about programming! By now, you know the basics of coding and how to use Scratch. You have the tools to create whatever you want! You can make things just for fun or for more useful purposes. For example, you could make a quiz to help you study for a test. Or you could create a how-to guide for how to make a really great paper airplane. You can even use Scratch to teach others about coding!

This is just the beginning for you. Now you know how to look at the whole world like a programmer, which means you can break down all sorts of problems and find logical solutions for them. You can use coding basics in all aspects of your life. Next time you have a task to complete, just think of how you can break it down into smaller steps to make it more manageable.

Need to fold the laundry? Instead of grabbing clothes randomly from the basket and making lots of stacks, come up with a step-by-step plan. Maybe you could sort all the clothes by type first and *then* fold. That way you wouldn't have to spend time looking for the right stack each time you fold a piece of clothing. Everything in your pile would already go together in the same stack! There's no limit to how you can think like a programmer and use your coding toolbox, on and off your computer.

Good luck on your coding journey,
and never stop learning!

# Bug Hunting: Troubleshooting Tips

All programmers are constantly checking for bugs and problem-solving their code. Here are some common mistakes that new coders make in Scratch and how to fix them! If you're having trouble coding the activities in this book, you can also view all the activities and play them on my website: **RainaBurditt.com**.

| Common Problem | Quick Solution |
|---|---|
| Program not starting | Make sure your code is attached to an event code block. All scripts must start with an event. |
| Sprite spins upside down | Use a *set rotation style (left-right)* motion block to keep the sprite from rotating. |
| Motion code not working | Make sure you have a *wait* control block between different motion blocks so there is time for you to see the movements. |
| Sprite disappeared and won't come back | Add a *show* looks block to the beginning of your script. |
| Costume changed but now sprite still has the second costume when program is restarted | Add a *switch costume to (__)* looks block to the beginning of your script to set the starting costume. |
| Backdrop changed but now program won't restart back with the original backdrop | Add a *switch backdrop to (__)* looks block at the beginning of your script to program the starting backdrop. |
| Broadcast not working | Try double-checking the name of the broadcast you sent out. If it doesn't match, that's why. |

| Common Problem | Quick Solution |
|---|---|
| Sprite receiving a broadcast over and over again | Check to see if you have sent a broadcast within a forever loop somewhere. Use a *stop (__)* control block to make the broadcast stop repeating. |
| Variable not changing | Try double-checking the name of the variable you selected to change. If it doesn't match, that's why. |
| Variable changing too quickly (Ex: multiple points scored for just one hit) | Add a *wait* control block after your *change (__) by (__)* variable block. |
| Sprite disappears from view | Click the "Show" button that looks like an eyeball under the stage. |
| List showing on the stage | Unclick the little box next to your list code block in your code menu or use the *hide list (__)* list block. |
| Variable is not showing on the stage | Click the little box next to your variable code block in your menu or use the *show variable (__)* variable block. |

When in doubt, pull your code apart and test each step one at a time to find the source of the problem. Be patient, and remember, even the experts have to check for bugs!

# Glossary

**algorithm:** Any logical set of steps used to perform a task or solve a problem

**Booleans:** Variables that have just two possible values, true or false

**broadcast:** A message sent out by one script that can be received by another script as a trigger

**bugs:** Errors in code that prevent a program from running properly

**code:** A list of instructions for a computer to follow

**code blocks:** Color-coded symbols that represent different commands that can be placed into the Scratch script editor to write a script

**code menu:** The list of possible code blocks in Scratch

**conditional execution:** Different paths that a computer can take based on rules that you set

**control block:** Code used in Scratch to adjust timing, create loops, or create conditionals

**coordinate plane:** An area formed by the intersection of a vertical line called the y-axis and a horizontal line called the x-axis

**coordinates:** The location of a point on a coordinate plane

**data:** Information

**data structure:** Different ways to organize information

**data types:** Different ways to express information, like numbers or strings

**debugging:** Working to find and fix problems in your code

**event block:** Code used in Scratch to start a new script

**event handling:** Messages to let your computer know to start following a particular set of directions, or script

**events:** Triggers that tell the computer to begin following a list of code

**function:** A piece of code that does not run unless it is triggered by certain input

**input:** Information entered into the computer by a user

**looks block:** Code used in Scratch to change how sprites and words appear on the screen

**loop:** A tool to create repetition in your code

**math:** Operations that a computer can perform for you

**motion block:** Code used in Scratch to make sprites move around

**offline:** Not connected to the Internet

**online:** Connected to the Internet

**operator block:** Code used in Scratch to set up math calculations and comparisons

**operators:** A special type of function that allows you to make math calculations like adding and subtracting

**output:** Information provided by the computer to the user

**program:** A set of directions for a computer to follow

**repetition:** The repeating action of a set of steps

**run:** Test code by starting the program

**script:** Code in a specific programming language

**script editor:** The area of Scratch where code blocks are placed to build a script

**sensing block:** Code used in Scratch to notice things such as the location of the user's mouse or when two sprites are touching

**sound block:** A coding block used in Scratch to add sounds to your program

**sprites:** Images (such as characters and items) in Scratch that can be coded to do things in a program

**stage:** The area of Scratch where you can preview your program

**strings:** Groups of characters or text

**variable block:** Code used in Scratch to create variables and change their values

**variables:** Containers that hold information and can have a changing value

**x-axis:** The horizontal line on a coordinate plane

**y-axis:** The vertical line on a coordinate plane

# Resources

## SCRATCH DISCUSSION FORUMS

Need help with your Scratch project? Ask here! You can pose your own questions or search discussions others have had about coding in Scratch. You can also help others find the bugs in their programs!

Scratch.MIT.edu/discuss

## HOUR OF CODE

If you're interested in learning even more coding languages, Hour of Code is a good place to test the waters! This nonprofit-run website includes a huge library of one-hour tutorials in lots of different programming languages. This is a great way to try out a new language to see if you would like to learn more about it.

HourOfCode.com/us

## CODE.ORG

This website is a collection of full coding courses for kids to teach you how to make your own games, apps, computer drawings, and websites.

Code.org

## CODECADEMY

When you're ready to level up, Codecademy is a great collection of more advanced coding courses. Check this out when you feel like you have conquered the rest!

Codecademy.com

# Index

## A

Algorithms, 6, 166
Arrow keys
    coding challenges, 89, 101
    conditions, using to control arrow keys, 99–100, 106
    down-arrow key, using to stop sprite, 87
    right-arrow key, using to increase sprite speed, 86
*Ask ( ) and wait* sensing block
    list blocks, adding to, 112, 113, 118
    password creation, using with, 95
    pop-up box, typing name into, 77–78
    questions, creating with, 147
    *when flag clicked* event block, connecting to, 83, 116

## B

Backdrops
    backdrops icon, 44, 47
    backdrops library, 48, 64
    hack for backdrop change during program, 53
    *switch backdrop to* looks block, 45, 95, 96, 147, 155, 164
Basic coding concepts, 5–6
Blue cat icon, 26, 43, 47
Booleans, 76, 96, 109, 166
Broadcasts
    broadcast event, how to send and receive, 127
    multiple broadcasts, practice in sending, 130–133
    new scripts, using broadcasts to run, 128, 134, 142
    Obstacle Course, applying to, 161
    quick solution for broadcast not working, 164
    receiving broadcasts, 137, 139, 140, 150, 151
    *stop ( )* control block, killing a broadcast with, 152
    troubleshooting tip for receiving a broadcast, 165
*Broadcast ( )* event block
    new message, creating for, 131
    signals, sending with, 126
    sprite size, using to change, 127
    timing of a program, adjusting with, 143
    as a trigger to set off the next action, 130
*Broadcast ( ) and wait* event block
    "I Had Help," naming block as, 118
    multiple broadcasts, creating with, 136
    "Return the Wand" broadcast event, setting up, 153–154
    "Start Game," naming block as, 148
    *stop ( )* control block, connecting to, 152
    timing of script, setting with, 135, 143
Bugs
    hack to check for bugs in multiple scripts, 39
    as mistakes in code, 23, 166
    troubleshooting tips, 164–165

events, launching by clicking an icon, 6, 13

hack for copying code to a new icon, 72

right-click to duplicate, 67

script editor, enter by clicking an icon, 48, 51, 60, 104, 127

show (eyeball) icon, 156, 165

sound icon, click to bring up sound library, 46

*See also* Green flag icon

Input, as information entered into the computer, 4, 7, 83, 85, 166

# L

Libraries

backdrops library, 44, 48, 64, 94

sounds library, 46-47, 52, 65

sprites library, 26, 43, 48, 62, 77, 94, 115

List blocks

*add (__) to (__)*, 112, 113, 147

*colors*, 118, 119

*delete (__) of (__)*, 113, 122

*hide list (__)*, 117, 118

*item (__) of (__)*, 116, 157

*replace item (__) of (__) with (__)*, 122

*show list (__)*, 118

Lists

coding challenge, 114

in Fire-Breathing Wand Quest!, 147

how to make a list, 111-112

multiple variables, lists allowing for storage of, 110

Variables section of code menu, new list option found in, 113, 115

Looks blocks

appearance of sprite, changing with, 20, 166

*change size by (__)*, 127, 128

*go to (__) layer*, 156

*hide*, 50, 69, 96, 140

*next costume*, 62, 63, 73, 98, 138

*switch backdrop to*, 45, 95, 96, 147, 155, 164

*See also Hide; Say (__) for (__) seconds; Set size to (__) %; Show; Switch costume to* looks blocks

Loops

broadcasts, troubleshooting tip to quit repeating, 165

coding challenge to create a backdrops loop, 66

conditions, setting up with, 100, 154

control blocks, using to loop, 21, 63, 71, 82, 88

in Fire-Breathing Wand Quest! activity, 148, 149-150, 152, 153

repetition, creating with, 6, 55-56, 59, 69, 167

# M

Math

math calculations, operator as a type of function allowing, 7, 167

as one of the five basic parts of a program, 4

operator blocks, setting up math calculations with, 21

Motion blocks

*change x by (__)*, 36, 38, 99, 149

*change y by (__)*, 36, 38, 64, 100

*move (__) steps (__)*, 62, 85

new coordinate numbers, updating blocks with, 32, 68

scripts, attaching to, 39

*set y to (__)*, 148, 149

sprite direction, switching with, 20, 30, 33, 87, 167

# S

*Say (__) for (__) seconds* looks block
  *answer* variable, using with, 120
  in Ask Wizard Toad, 116
  in Fire-Breathing Wand Quest!, 148, 153, 156, 157
  in Knock, Knock!, 130, 131, 132
  in Mission: Donuts!, 104
  password creation, using in, 96, 97
  repeat loop, placing after, 82
  in Talk to a Sprite, 78–79
  word bubbles, using to create, 122

Scoring. *See* Game scores

Scratch
  benefits of using, 8, 9
  offline installation, 12–13
  online installation, 13–14
  saving work, 16–17
  share project, how to, 15
  start and stop a program, how to, 14, 16, 17, 19
  as a visual programming language, 7, 20

Scratch Desktop, 12–13, 15, 17, 25

Scratch the Cat, 18, 19, 26

Script editor
  assembling a program in, 18, 62, 63
  Code tab, clicking to bring up script editor, 42, 52
  in Dodge the Stars activity, 67–69
  dragging code blocks from code menu to, 19, 31
  duplicating code, checking in a sprite's script editor after, 72
  extra code, deleting from, 35
  in Fire-Breathing Wand Quest! activity, 147–150, 153–157
  in Flying Ball Thief activity, 136–138, 140
  glossary definition, 167

  icons, clicking to bring up a sprite's script editor, 48, 51, 60, 104, 127
  in Knock, Knock! activity, 130–133
  in Sneak Past the Shark activity, 84–87
  *when flag clicked* event block, dragging into, 57, 95, 102

Scripts
  costume options, switching in script, 42
  creating scripts, 19
  defining, 7
  event code blocks, beginning scripts with, 22
  multiple scripts, testing individually, 39
  *when flag clicked* event block, starting a script with, 51, 95
  Your First Script activity, 31–34

Sensing blocks
  *answer*, 95, 112, 119, 147
  coding challenge, 79
  defining, 21, 167
  *key (__) pressed?*, 99, 100
  *mouse y* sensing command, 148, 149
  Obstacle Course, option for using in, 161
  text bubble, dragging sensing blocks into, 78
  *touching (__) ?*, 102, 151, 154
  *See also Ask (__) and wait* sensing block

*Set rotation style (left-right)* motion block
  in Fire-Breathing Wand Quest! activity, 150
  opposite direction, making sprite move in, 33, 87, 130, 136, 155
  rotation options, 30
  sprite spinning upside down, troubleshooting remedy for, 164

*Set size to (__) %* looks block
  motion blocks, adding after, 149, 150
  preset sprite size, adjusting, 49, 57, 98, 102, 137

in Flying Ball Thief activity, 135
game timer, how to create, 80–82
in Go, Llama, Go! activity, 36–38
in Home Run Hitter activity, 51

# V

Variables
*answer* variable, connecting with operator
blocks, 120
Boolean as a type of variable, 96
*change (__) by (__)* variable, 81, 86, 151
as changeable, 75, 110
in Fire-Breathing Wand Quest! activity,
152, 153
information, storing with, 77–78, 110, 122
*my variable* button, option to use, 80
as one of the five basic parts of a
program, 5
*show variable (__)* variable block, 150
speed of sprites, adjusting with variables,
84–85, 87
string variable, 76, 91
variable code blocks, creating with, 21

# W

*Wait (__) seconds* control block
Control code menu, as found in, 37
default time, adjusting, 51, 58, 59, 62, 63,
70, 98, 138
*hide* looks block, adding to, 60, 69, 88, 103
loop creation, using in, 59, 88
motion blocks, connecting with, 38, 67
*next costume* looks block, placing after,
62, 98, 138
removing block, experimenting with, 68
*switch costume to (__)* looks blocks,
placing between, 51, 58, 63, 151
timer, using in construction of, 81

*When flag clicked* event block
beginning a script with, 63, 125, 147
control blocks, adding to, 31, 51, 99
Events code menu, as found in, 31
list blocks, connecting with, 81, 103, 113,
117, 118
looks blocks, placing after, 49, 68, 77, 95,
138, 154, 155
motion blocks, adding to, 57, 67, 84,
130, 136
resizing command, connecting with, 57,
98, 102, 137
sensing blocks, placing after, 77, 83, 116
sound block, adding to, 65
unhooking code from, 35, 59
variable blocks, connecting with, 81, 103
*When I receive (__)* event block
control blocks, connecting with to create a
condition, 152, 153
looks blocks, placing after, 131, 149, 150,
155, 156
multiple scripts with same trigger, setting
up, 138
new scripts, starting with, 126, 137, 139,
140, 151, 157
shrink command, sprite receiving, 127
Start Game option, choosing from drop-
down menu, 148
triggering a response with, 132
Word bubbles, 20, 109, 122

# X

X- and y-coordinates
coordinate plane, moving sprites along, 27
new sprite positions, coordinates changing
with, 28–29
whole numbers as used for, 109
y-axis, moving sprite along, 64

# About the Author

**Raina Burditt, MS, MA** started coding for fun after participating in an Hour of Code activity using Scratch. Even though she was an English teacher, she found a way to work coding into her class. Her seventh graders loved using Scratch to code scenes from the novel they were studying! She was very inspired by their enthusiasm and creativity. Raina has an MA in English Literature and an MS in Instructional Design & Technology, and her passion for computers finally led her to decide to become a technology teacher! Now she works with seventh through twelfth graders on a variety of technology skills, and she also works with teachers in all subjects, helping them integrate technology into their teaching.

Check out her website: **RainaBurditt.com**. You can find links to the activities in this book as well as other coding resources.